Decision Making
in Developing Countries

Alfredo Sfeir-Younis
Daniel W. Bromley

The Praeger Special Studies program—
utilizing the most modern and efficient book
production techniques and a selective
worldwide distribution network—makes
available to the academic, government, and
business communities significant, timely
research in U.S. and international economic, social, and political development.

Decision Making in Developing Countries

Multiobjective Formulation and Evaluation Methods

PRAEGER SPECIAL STUDIES IN INTERNATIONAL ECONOMICS AND DEVELOPMENT

Praeger Publishers   New York   London

Library of Congress Cataloging in Publication Data

Sfeir-Younis, Alfredo, 1947-
    Decision making in developing countries.

    (Praeger special studies in international economics
and development)
    Bibliography: p.
    Includes index.
    1. Underdeveloped areas. 2. Decision-making—
Mathematical models. I. Bromley, Daniel W.,
1940-   joint author. II. Title.
HC59.7.S4458   1977   338.91'172'4   77-9636
ISBN 0-03-022286-9

PRAEGER SPECIAL STUDIES
200 Park Avenue, New York, N.Y., 10017, U.S.A.

Published in the United States of America in 1977
by Praeger Publishers,
A Division of Holt, Rinehart and Winston, CBS, Inc.

789   038   987654321

To

Mary Lola and Joyce

Goal programming is capable of depicting the decision-making process in developing countries as consisting of several steps. The first step is the identification of planning targets or objectives. The second step is the assessment of the means to achieve those objectives. The third step is the assignment of weights to the various objectives based upon some politically specified preference ordering— a form of a social welfare function. The fourth step is the assignment of weights to the over- or underachievement of the relevant targets. From this one can discuss the optimal investment portfolio under the assumption of projects which are either perfectly divisible or perfectly indivisible (lumpy). The sixth step is the simulation of the impacts, over time, on the selected targets—national income, regional income, foreign exchange earnings, national employment, regional employment, and so on.

This book is based on research concerned with exploring the usefulness of goal programming for decision making in developing countries. Its intellectual roots lie in a general dissatisfaction with the project-by-project application of rather traditional benefit-cost analysis in developing countries. Part of this dissatisfaction arises from the fact that a single metric—a benefit-cost ratio, or a figure depicting present-valued net benefits—often conceals more than it reveals about the full range of impacts arising from one or more projects. This feeling of unease is reinforced by our experience in developing countries where national planning is at odds with this piecemeal approach to evaluating isolated investments. Thus, our intent here is to attempt a rather general description of investment decision making in the developing countries, and then to explore the ways in which goal programming might usefully be incorporated therein.

We do not pretend that this small effort represents the definitive work on goal programming or on development planning. We do maintain that it constitutes a useful integration of the two areas. Its purpose is merely to introduce planners and economists interested in decision making in the developing countries to an important quantitative technique which enjoys some currency in multiobjective decision making by business firms. It is our hypothesis that its usefulness will be much appreciated by those who daily struggle with the difficult problem of reconciling the many projects which filter up from "action" agencies with the larger economic planning offices and ministries of finance.

This book grows out of joint work over a period of several years while Alfredo Sfeir-Younis was a doctoral candidate in the Department of Agricultural Economics at the University of Wisconsin. It is impossible to pay adequate tribute to the many individuals who provided valuable assistance over that period. First, however, we wish to express our grateful appreciation for financial assistance provided in the form of a doctoral dissertation fellowship for Sfeir-Younis from Resources of the Future, Washington, D.C. Our intellectual debts to the following individuals are great: Richard Bishop, Wilfred Candler, Pierre Crosson, Ronald Cummings, William Dobson, David B. Johnson, Leon Mears, John Schmidt, John Strasma, and Robert Young. Their assistance, at various times over the past four years, is greatly appreciated. Finally, we are indeed grateful for the generous typing assistance of Mary Davis, Julie Peters, Mary Schmiesing, and Marcia Verhage, and for the artwork of Karen Rittenhouse.

CONTENTS

Page

PREFACE   vii

LIST OF TABLES   xii

LIST OF FIGURES   xiv

Chapter

1   THE CONCEPTUAL IMPERATIVE   1

    The Decision-making Problem   1
    An Overview   6
    References   7

2   A MULTIOBJECTIVE INVESTMENT FORMU-
    LATION METHOD FOR POLICY MAKERS IN
    DEVELOPING COUNTRIES   9

    Investment Planning   9
    Evaluators and Policy Makers   11
    The Model   17
    Summary   21
    References   21

3   INVESTMENT CRITERIA FOR CAPITAL
    BUDGETING DECISIONS   24

    Budgeting Individual Projects   24
    Capital Budgeting and Mathematical
        Programming   30
    Summary   40
    References   41

4   MATHEMATICAL FORMULATION OF THE
    MODEL: VECTOR OPTIMIZATION AND GOAL
    PROGRAMMING   44

Multiobjective Optimization and Goal
   Programming   44
The Model   48
Policy Maker's Objectives: The Choice
   of a Distance Function   54
Characteristics of Decisions and Modeling
   Options   56
Dealing with Uncertainty   62
Time as an Endogenous Variable   70
The Utility Approach to Project Formulation   71
Summary   77
References   77

5   BASIS FOR A DATA SYSTEM   80

Investment-Opportunity Matrix   81
Source-of-Funds Matrix   94
Summary   98
References   99

6   THE ECONOMICS OF PROJECT FINANCING   102

The Method   107
Optimal Currency Mix   107
Foreign-Aid Management   118
Fund Disbursement, or the Economics of
   Project Implementation   122
Summary   127
References   128

7   PROGRAM FORMULATION: AN EXAMPLE   129

Project Formulation   132
Constrained Formulation   152
Summary   154
References   157

8   PUBLIC INVESTMENTS AND BALANCED
     DEVELOPMENT POLICIES: AN EXAMPLE   158

A Hierarchical Model   159
Government as a Rule Maker: An Example   167
Summary   175
References   176

Chapter   Page

    9   CONCLUSIONS   177

BIBLIOGRAPHY   182

INDEX   195

ABOUT THE AUTHORS   201

LIST OF TABLES

Table		Page
3.1	Capital Outlay and NPV of Alternative Investments	33
6.1	Hypothetical Project Cash Flows and Loan Repayment Schedule	110
6.2	Source-of-Funds Matrix and Goal Vector	120
6.3	Ranking Sources of Funds	121
7.1	Information Needs for Investment Formulation: Investment-Opportunity Matrix and Goal Vector	131
7.2	Information Needs for Investment Formulation: Source-of-Funds Matrixes	134
7.3	Information Needs for Investment Formulation: Weights for Sensitivity Analysis	135
7.4	Optimal Investment Strategy under the Assumption of Perfect Divisibility and Undistinguishable Budget in $t = 0$	137
7.5	Optimal Investment Strategy under Different Assumptions Concerning Budget, Goals, and Weights	139
7.6	Vector of Preferences for Urban Location	141
7.7	Solution Vector Given $\Sigma x_j = 1$, and Ranking Public Investment by the Reduced-Cost Method	142
7.8	Macroeconomic Impacts of the Investment Strategies Developed in Table 7.5	144
7.9	Macroeconomic Impacts of the Optimal Investment Strategy When Total Acceptance or Rejection of Projects Is Assumed	148
7.10	Technical Coefficients of Employment Reflecting Locational Impacts of Projects	149

Table		Page
7.11	Optimal Investment Strategy and Macro-economic Impacts with Spatial Location Effects of Projects	150
7.12	Expected Value of Generated Employment with $p = .25$	151
7.13	Optimal Investment Strategies under Different Assumptions Relative to the Value of p (probability) Using W_6 from Table 7.3	152
7.14	Optimal Investment Strategy and Macro-economic Impacts under Constrained Formulation	155
8.1	Attributes of Project X_5	163
8.2	Impact of Interest Rate and Depreciation Policies upon the Optimal Investment Bundle and Macroeconomic Contributions	171
8.3	Significance of Rule-making Alternatives upon the Optimal Investment Strategy and Macro-economic Contributions	173

LIST OF FIGURES

Figure		Page
2.1	Investment Planning: A Flow-Chart Diagram	12
2.2	Multiobjective-Hierarchical Investment Decision Model	18
2.3	The Economics of Project Financing	20
3.1	Fractional Projects and Budget Utilization	39
4.1	Decision and Functional Space	47
4.2	The Graphic Solution of Goal Programming	53
4.3	Topological Convergency of Different Distance Functions, an Illustration in a Normalized Two-Dimensional Space: $X_1 \varepsilon$ [-1, 1]; $X_2 \varepsilon$ [-1, 1]	55
4.4	Introduction of Deviational Variables: A Geometric Interpretation	57
4.5	Utility over the Attributes: Feasible Region	73
4.6	Utility over the Attributes: Direction of Preferences	74
6.1	The Financing Process	104
6.2	The Economics of Project Financing	108
6.3	Different Lengths of Time for Constructing a Project	124
6.4	Time Paths of Project Attributes	126
7.1	Policy-maker Level of Decision Making: First Level of Decision Making Assumed Constant	130
7.2	Employment Levels under Different Assumptions of Objective Weights and Budget	145

Figure   Page

7.3   Regional Income Levels under Different Assump-
       tions of Objective Weights and Budget   146

7.4   Foreign-Exchange Levels under Different
       Assumptions of Weights and Budget   147

7.5   Macroeconomic Impact of Projects for Different
       Values of p (probability of employment
       generation)   153

7.6   Macroeconomic Impacts of Alternative Invest-
       ment Bundles: Assumption of Project Perfect
       Divisibility   156

8.1   The Hierarchical Model   166

8.2   Production Implications of Different Combina-
       tions of Interest Rates and Depreciation
       (i, d) for Project X_5 168

8.3   Shadow-profit Implications of Different Combina-
       tions of Interest Rates and Depreciation (i, d)
       for Project X_5 169

8.4   Macroeconomic Impacts of Various Interest
       Rate and Depreciation Policies   172

Decision Making
in Developing Countries

1

THE CONCEPTUAL
IMPERATIVE

THE DECISION-MAKING PROBLEM

For the year 1974—the latest in which reliable figures are
available—the foreign debt of 86 developing countries totaled $151
billion. This represents an increase of $30 billion over 1973, and
some analysts fear that for 1976 the figure may be $200 billion.
While there is little consensus that this debt portends an international
monetary crisis, there is serious concern for those developing
countries not blessed with significant oil deposits. The recent
worldwide recession, widespread inflation in world food and petroleum
markets, and various currency adjustments place many of the developing nations in a very precarious economic position.

As this situation continues, and as developing nations move
toward greater emphasis on social overhead projects—schools,
communications, highways, health and nutrition, general rural
development—it becomes imperative that economic analysis of
public actions reflects the basic climate in which investment decisions are made. The conventional approach is often characterized
by an undue emphasis on project-by-project evaluation using rather
conventional benefit-cost analysis.

On a theoretical level, investment evaluation discussions
generally start by making a distinction between financial feasibility
and economic feasibility; the former being concerned with repayment
capacity and usually dismissed as inappropriate for social decision
making. The implication then is, though never made explicit, that
the broader economic evaluation of investments results in choices
which are socially preferred. This serious confusion of Pareto
optimality (economic efficiency) with social optimality results in
delusion on the part of decision makers. Economic efficiency is

elevated to a conceptually invalid level in the social milieu, and the economist assumes a high-priest function of often antisocial proportions; the actual role of the state and the place of economic evaluation therein becomes greatly distorted (Bromley 1976).

The achievement of a socially preferred state of the economy, as a result of approving a given investment activity, might be approached by considering four different types of objectives: (1) to maximize a given social welfare function $W = W(W_1, \ldots, W_n)$, designating as the most socially preferred state that with the largest $\triangle W$; (2) to qualify the socially preferred state as that one in which "everybody wins" ($\triangle W_i > 0$); (3) to qualify the socially preferred state as the one in which "someone wins, nobody loses" ($\triangle W_i \geq 0$); and (4) to qualify the socially preferred state as one in which "the winners outweigh the losers" (Hinrichs 1969).

These objectives have been considered to answer two central questions: (1) if an investment project transforms an economic state I (Z_1) into an economic state II (Z_2), is Z_2 socially preferred? and (2) is it possible to achieve Z_2 merely by enforcing the Pareto allocative efficiency criterion? In order to answer question 1 we must decide what type of objective function is the most appropriate for determining the socially preferred state of the economy. Most economic analysis follows "the winners outweigh the losers"–the finding of a potential net gain (in benefit-cost analysis, a net present value greater than zero). This move to a potentially preferred state requires a further decision: at what prices or set of revealed preferences will this gain be measured? The Kaldor criterion measures the gain before the move to Z_2, Hicks measures it after the move, and Scitovsky measures it at both. The usual statement is that if the Kaldor-Hicks and Scitovsky criteria are satisfied, a move from Z_1 to Z_2 will represent a potential increase in welfare in the absence of a social welfare function (Bergson-Samuelson index of well-being).

One of the major limitations of the Pareto proposition, and of benefit-cost analysis and its practical application to allocation theory, is the ignored changes in the distribution of income. In other words, passing from Z_1 to Z_2 as a potentially Pareto preferred state (efficient) may move the economy to a distributionally inferior state (see Mishan [1969] for a detailed discussion of this issue).

Even the familiar and relatively well-accepted concept of positive net present-valued (NPV) benefits (or a benefit-cost ratio in excess of unity) satisfies only the potential compensation test. That is, the existence of NPV benefits is merely assurance that the gainers could compensate the losers from a given public-sector activity. In the absence of a unanimity rule, where approval could be obtained from all only with actual compensation, the potential compensation test suffers from three crucial weaknesses. That is, the revered Pareto criteria (1) ignores completely distributional considerations—indeed it sanctifies the current distribution; (2) is inconclusive (Scitovsky); and (3) is consistent with only one person being made better off, and all others being made worse off (again, see Mishan [1969] for an evaluation of the relative strengths and weakness of the four possible criteria).

The traditional fascination with optimality and efficiency results in the practice of first worrying about efficient investments, and then dealing—or pretending to deal—with the distributional issues. However, the prevailing set of rights, endowments, and relative prices dictates the position and elasticity of demand and supply curves and hence constrains the Pareto-optimal configuration; change rights, initial endowments, or relative prices and the optimal configuration changes. There is no unique efficient solution but an infinity of efficient solutions depending upon the institutional structure of society. This statement has specific implications for sound investment planning. Project/program investment planning makes no sense without appropriate and effective institutional policies; irrigation projects without adequate water laws; increasing aggregate output levels without distribution policies; creation of wealth without opening new access to it; development of public ownership without foreign investment policy; employment programs without a policy about new technologies are all examples. To assume that projects by themselves will create the expected development environment will only favor the existing status quo, or will exacerbate current inequities in income and power.

This leads the economist to consider question 2. This question not only touches upon the attainment of a given allocative efficiency, but on the achievement of a desired pattern of distribution. This can also be stated by saying that society will improve its welfare if Pareto efficiency is really realized (NVP > 0) and there is an institutional structure which will allow the gainers to compensate the losers. Samuelson (1969, p. 419) calls this potential achievement of an actual improvement the "political feasibility" of welfare economics by stating that "we could move people to different points on the utility-possibility function only by an ideally perfect and unattainable system of absolutely lump-sum taxes or subsidies."

Given these institutional preconditions to attain not only a given pattern of distribution of income but to achieve an economic state of better allocative efficiency, it is necessary to define some structural connotations of the allocation mechanism of investment projects and the different courses of action that follow. This will help to explain the failure by structure of many project evaluation decision-making models.

These elements have specific implications for the application of investment planning models. Our model offers planners the opportunity to select investments in a multiobjective context, it can guide planners on the importance of institutional arrangements, and it gives assistance on the economics of project financing. We could leave the policy maker at that stage (state Z_2 "socially" preferred to Z_1), distribute the government budget based on the accepted projects, and forget about our institutional matrix. Yet it is the policy options at the project level, the definition of target groups, the creation of employment, and the like which constitute the dynamics of development. This dynamic will materialize if and only if the proper creation of and access to substantial flows of wealth are achieved.

A decision to move to Z_2 (socially preferred to Z_1) may consider (1) an allocation mechanism (do not confuse with market mechanism) in which the institutional arrangements are mostly in accord with the physical relationships of the system; or (2) an economic state in which the allocation mechanism is not in accord with the options and structure rationalized by a model. This second situation will attract most of our attention. Situation 2 may be caused basically by the consistent but rather misleading desire to obtain maximum "efficiency." This misconception negates the basic relationship between the attainment of specified efficiency levels in the allocation and distribution of resources and the given set of rights: different sets of rights determine different sets of relative prices and, then, different efficient solutions to the system. In this case, the lack of consideration of the appropriate role of institutions in their allocation and distribution of resources prevents the system from moving to the socially preferred state. This situation can be called one of perverse rights as opposed to situation 1 which can be called one of neutral rights. In situation 1 the allocation mechanism does not cause fiscal infeasibility; for any allocative rule there are institutionally enforceable rules compatible with the "optimal" solution.

This discussion draws attention to the dual roles of government: as an investor and as a rule maker; in our view the extensive literature on development planning and investment (project) evaluation has had the effect of subordinating the most important role of government (that of rule maker) in the economist's discussion of development. The output-creating aspects of traditional growth models seem to have converted development into a one-factor problem where the relation between the rate of growth of income to savings relative to capital-output ratios provides the main conceptual mind set. The plethora of investment planning manuals and project evaluation books (guides) would lead one to believe that the efficient selection of investments is not only necessary but is sufficient for economic growth and development.

For traditional planners, investment in the context of economic
development involves five basic principles: (1) accumulation principle: there is a direct relationship between development and investment; (2) interrelation principle: there must be an organization
planning structure to coordinate the development alternatives; (3)
acceleration principle: a structure that allows for "rapid" development; (4) consistency principle: this structure for economic development should be such that the identification of society's objectives is
made through the development planning process; and (5) sacrifice
principle: the impossibility of simultaneously satisfying all of the
objectives (United Nations 1963). While we recognize the existence
and need for an appropriate integration of these traditional principles
at the formulation stage, it is also important to consider an institutional principle. This recognizes the possibility of having development without increasing the set of investments. In this case,
development is associated with the identification of the appropriate
institutional changes and self-generating economic incentives within
a given developmental environment. The institutional principle
reinforces, then, not only the role of government as goal setter and
investor or producer (that is, spending), but also as regulator and
fiscal agent (that is, rule making). Institutional constraints and
their relaxation—rules and the possibility for their change—are often
(badly) referred to as mere administrative or organizational matters.
But, it is this distribution of laws, working rules (such as price
supports, tariff policies, and so on), rights, and the exposure to the
power of others which is at the heart of bringing about different
behavior which might enhance the economic position of the majority
of a country's citizens.

By way of summary, it is important to recognize a crucial
distinction between stocks and flows in investment decision making.
The project-by-project approach to investment decision making
creates an inordinate concentration on stocks and often overlooks
the flow aspects which are so crucial to sustained development.
Stocks and flows are not independent. This is another element that
must be presented to policy makers when analyzing alternative institutional arrangements; the magnitude of the flow effect is a function
of the existing stock and vice versa. The magnitude of one effect
will determine the magnitude and time required (acceleration) to
put the other in action. In general, when the size of the stock is
very large relative to the generated flow, changes in the stock resulting from the flow are typically small.

A measure of performance of a given set of institutions might
be defined by its ratio between the flow effect (FE) over its stock
effect (SE) (Branson 1970). This information must be presented
to the policy maker with an implicit rule of choosing that one which

has the highest ratio FE/SE. We say "implicit" because there are
other considerations such as the social cost of changing any particular
institution; a given institutional arrangement may be feasible but
socially unacceptable.

It is this flow component which leads us to construct a decision-
making framework which places considerable emphasis on the
achievement of certain social goals (targets) over time. It is these
goals which occupy policy makers in developing countries; the usual
gap between plan formulation based on macroeconomic targets and
project selection based on traditional efficiency criteria is reflected
in the frequent reformulation, reselection, and rejection of projects
which others, at a "lower" level in the decision system, consider
"good." The approach taken here is intended to overcome that gap,
and to illustrate a decision model which will facilitate that end.

AN OVERVIEW

Chapter 2 presents a general overview of the decision-making
model. Chapter 3 begins by introducing general capital-budgeting
approaches; this is the tradition out of which grew multiobjective
decision models. Chapter 4 turns to a detailed specification of the
decision model and illustrates how the model is operated within a
goal programming framework. It is here that we can illustrate how
the model is helpful to policy makers for (1) the determination of
project priorities in terms of the optimal investment bundle; (2) the
macroeconomic impacts of various projects over their respective
lives; and (3) the allocation of the government investment budget,
including both domestic and foreign funds. The model permits three
possible approaches to the determination of the optimal investment
bundle. That is, we can operate in terms of total acceptance or
rejection of specific projects, we can ascertain the optimal level
(fraction) of financing for each project, and we can determine the
optimal ranking of projects.

We can thus highlight the stock/flow aspect by deriving the
optimal investment bundle, the stock; and can then ascertain the
macroeconomic impacts, the flow. Another important aspect of the
decision model is the incorporation of guidance on project financing.
We will offer assistance on three important problems: (1) the optimal
currency mix—foreign versus domestic financing—for each project;
(2) the ranking and selecting from a number of foreign sources of
funds; and (3) guidance in terms of the disbursement of funds to
various aspects of a given project. This development is contained
in Chapter 6.

Returning to Chapter 5, the basis of the decision model is two matrixes containing the essential data about alternative investment opportunities and sources of funds. That is, we present an investment-opportunity matrix and a source-of-funds matrix which form the heart of the goal programming model. In the investment-opportunity matrix one arrays the various investment opportunities and their respective contribution over time to the set of prespecified planning goals (objectives, targets). Even without the formal model this informational array can be extremely useful to the policy maker, particularly in terms of stock and flow attributes. The source-of-funds matrix depicts alternative sources of financial assistance and the statistical characteristics of the loans. Here we are concerned with such factors as interest rate, grace period, maturity, flexibility, and the like.

Chapters 7 and 8 turn to actual implementation of the decision model using hypothetical data for an array of investment possibilities. The interest in Chapter 7 is with program formulation in that we are concerned with optimal investment strategies under different assumptions of preferences, goal vectors, and budget availability—and also with the level of goal accomplishment of different investment bundles. We are also concerned with the problem of constrained program formulation which arises, quite frequently, when one or more projects are imposed in the investment program for strictly political reasons. Here it is a problem of formulating the "discretionary" portion of the remaining investment budget; making the "best of a bad situation."

In Chapter 8 the concern is with public investments and balanced development policies as influenced by the rule-making role of government. That is, in Chapter 8 the interest will be with a decision process in which accomplishment of a goal vector is a function of an investment budget, and vectors of goals and weights. Here are explored alternative institutions—rules—given a rather fixed set of investment alternatives. Some institutional changes considered are those that pertain to the export component of one (or more) projects, the exchange rate for input and output, the interest rate and depreciation policies employed, the foreign price of an input, and the foreign price of an output. Throughout Chapter 8 there is emphasis on the rule-making role of government and the possibilities for significant development without investment.

REFERENCES

Branson, William H. 1970. "Monetary Policy and the New View of International Capital Movements." Brookings Papers on Economic Destiny, no. 2.

Bromley, Daniel W. 1976. "Economics and Public Decisions:
Roles of the State and Issues in Economic Evaluation." Journal
of Economic Issues 10 (December): 811-38.

Hinrichs, Harley H. 1969. "Government Decision Making and the
Theory of Benefit-Cost Analysis: A Primer." In Program
Budgeting and Benefit-Cost Analysis, ed. H. H. Hinrichs and
L. Taylor. Pacific Palisades, Calif.: Goodyear Publishing.

Mishan, E. J. 1969. Welfare Economics, Ten Introductory Lectures.
New York: Random House.

Samuelson, Paul A. 1969. "Evaluation of Real National Income."
In Readings in Welfare Economics, ed. K. Snow and T. Scitovsky.
Homewood, Ill.: Richard Irwin.

United Nations. 1963. Planning for Economic Development. New
York: United Nations.

2

A MULTIOBJECTIVE INVESTMENT FORMULATION METHOD FOR POLICY MAKERS IN DEVELOPING COUNTRIES

It often seems that there are more people (with different objectives) deciding the worthiness of investments than there are investments. In each country there are project formulators, project evaluators, and policy makers. Ciriacy-Wantrup (1971) has characterized them by three decision-making levels: operating level, institutional level, and policy level. Steiss (1972) classifies the plethora of decision makers as they fit into three different planning procedures: strategic planners, management planners, and operational planners. The first group is interested in the question of objectives, goals, and means, the second deals with the necessary tactical procedures to accomplish these objectives, and the third is concerned with scheduling and control.

It is not our intention to explore the merits or shortcomings of the numerous ways development planning procedures and decision makers have been characterized. Instead we present a model to help one group of decision makers formulate and select the optimal investment for the economy. That is, our primary interest lies with policy makers in the developing countries. The method or procedure to make the appropriate investment selection in developing countries will be developed in a model which permits illumination of, and planning with respect to, the objectives of this particular group.

INVESTMENT PLANNING

Public investment planning procedures are different in each developing nation. However, there are sufficient similarities to permit some generalizations. We do not intend to characterize the planning process in its formal and informal behavioral characteristics, but we need to establish a place for our model within this process.

Most developing nations have national budget offices (NBO), usually within the ministry of finance, in charge of allocating the government budget to different ministries and decentralized agencies. This budget will serve two macrofinancial purposes: (1) to implement services already in operation or new ones such as police, justice, city cleaning, supervision, and the like; and (2) to implement old and new programs and/or public investments for economic development. In the final analysis, the model developed here will assist in selecting a group of projects—the "optimal" investment strategy for the economy—and a budget for services and programs in a given sequence.

These investment alternatives are brought to the executive office (EO) by different ministries as proposals for financial implementation. There is a distinct variety of investments—roads, irrigation, projects, factories—brought by the respective ministries.

Who are those bringing proposals to the EO? One group that usually identifies and prepares projects in a particular ministry is the decentralized agency in the field supervising or implementing particular programs. Investment proposals might originate at the level of communities, municipalities, and districts. These entities may identify projects based upon their immediate needs, based upon an interpretation of government objectives, or to satisfy specific interest groups represented in the local government bodies. Another group that brings projects forward is politicians interpreting the "needs" of clients or their political parties; they bring them through the existing legislative branch (parliament). Another group that identifies and prepares investments is technicians who work in different ministries, departments, or on advisory committees and proceed by first interpreting the targets and goals of their executives.

Government budget allocation follows a specific time cycle with deadlines and procedures for when and how this budget should be allocated. At the presidential or prime-ministerial level (the EO), there is usually a central planning office (CPO) which is responsible for the appraisal of these projects and presentation to policy makers of the "optimal investment strategy," or the national plan. The CPO is usually an organization of economists, sociologists, and engineers who perform the role of formulating and evaluating—as separate entities or as one unit—these projects. Project evaluators receive projects from the project formulators who use not only technical data (that is, engineering, economics) but also the assessment of national priorities as they interpret CPO and EO objectives.

Then, project evaluators select projects based on "factual information" and "national parameters," the latter being the rate

of discount, social prices, and the like. The former is information
about the marginal propensity to consume of certain groups (or the
government), investment propensities of the private sector in a
particular economic activity, and so on (United Nations 1972).

Once projects have been appraised they usually go to the policy
makers, who might be an economic committee, an advisory group
to the president, or the governing party's central committee. The
selected projects are sent back to the executive office and/or ministries for financing. However, before there is a final agreement
about specific projects in the economy's portfolio, and the allocation
of domestic and foreign resources, the proposed plan may go to the
legislative branch of the country. After a period of time, and given
the parliamentary power of representatives and senators and the
veto power of the EO, there is a final decision on what should be the
optimal allocation of government resources and the investment strategy which would bring the maximum benefits to the economy. A flow
diagram that represents this selection process is presented in
Figure 2.1. While this may be a fair representation of the investment planning process in developing countries, there is no unique
representation for every developing country. In some countries
project evaluators, formulators, and policy makers are the same
group, although frequently evaluators and formulators do not play
the role of policy makers. We will treat them as a separate group.

EVALUATORS AND POLICY MAKERS

We start with a presentation of one of the CPO's functions which
has not been discussed in describing the investment planning procedures, nor in the models applied by the evaluators. The CPO prepares national and sectoral income accounts, balance-of-payments
accounts, sources and distribution of funds (domestic and foreign)
for the economy, and studies how previous accounts would be distributed among different economic activities (agriculture versus industry,
public versus private, domestic versus foreign) and among regions
of the country. This might be done on an ex-post basis, or projections might be based upon a given economic development pattern
sought by the policy makers. Moreover, the CPO often uses these
aggregate models to assess the levels of some merit-want parameters—
qualitative and quantitative economic, political, or institutional
objectives—which are very important for policy makers. These are
factors such as redistribution of wealth and income, achievement of
certain predetermined levels of employment, producing and saving
a given growth rate of national income, and the like. To understand
how this fits into the investment selection procedures we must clearly

FIGURE 2.1

Investment Planning: A Flow–Chart Diagram

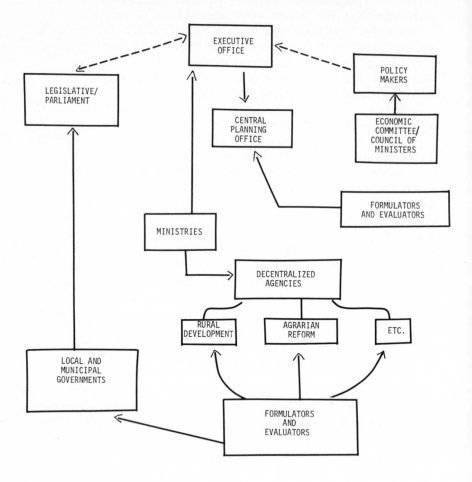

<u>Source</u>: Compiled by the author.

differentiate between two important decision makers: the evaluators and the policy makers.

Evaluators use a budgeting procedure that is conceptualized within a specific level of aggregation; projects are selected by using benefit–cost analysis (BCA). Here, projects are selected by their profitability to the economy on a project-by-project basis. BCA offers a particular level of aggregation which focuses on individual projects. For the most part, the economic literature has focused on developing investment manuals that help evaluators (economist/

planners) select an appropriate set of investments. These projects
are then passed to the policy makers who, sometimes, accept the
investment strategy proposed by evaluators and present it to the
parliament, or reject part of them, or introduce new projects which
were not considered nor selected to be "acceptable."

The policy maker works at a different level of aggregation which
implies a different perspective for selecting projects. First, the
policy maker is interested in appraising an optimal investment
strategy based on project characteristics to accomplish specific
developmental goals.* These characteristics will be defined differently depending upon the policy maker's objectives. We have chosen
characteristics which are quantifiable but which refer directly to
developing country development objectives; these are such factors
as employment, income, foreign exchange, and the like. In spite of
the fact that policy makers recognize the importance of appraising
projects based upon "efficiency" criteria, and on a project-by-project
basis, there is an increasing demand for models that take into account
the accomplishment of prespecified macroeconomic targets. This,
then, calls for an integration of investment selection models with
macroeconomic accounts and projections of the economy.

A dichotomy between project selection at the evaluator's level
and at the policy maker's level still persists in many developing
nations. To quote Sachs (1970, p. 34):

> In many countries there seems to be a gap between
> national development planning (including overall indus-
> trial planning), on the one hand, and programming
> at the project level. The national development plan
> is usually formulated [by policy makers] in terms
> of objectives involving such considerations as the
> standard of living, the average rate of growth, the
> level of employment, self-reliance, and distribution
> of income. In other words, the national plan is formu-
> lated in terms of broad categories of over-all national
> objectives. Although individual projects [selected by
> evaluators] are developed within the broad framework
> of the plan (and sectoral programs), the gap between
> national planning [policy maker] and that at the project
> level [evaluator] is, in most cases, not bridged.

---

*Lancaster (1971) first introduced characteristics of commodities
rather than individual commodities in consumption analysis. One
application to public decision making has been made by Sandmo (1973),
and recently by Maslove (1976).

Policy makers will select that investment bundle which will be closest to the complete accomplishment of their developmental objectives. These characteristics will be related to the nation's objectives and will be programmed in direct relation to targets and projections set by national income and balance-of-payment models.

The basic nature of social objectives is their multiplicity and conflicting interrelationships. The objectives for formulation of the optimal investment strategy for economic development may be defined as specific statements of what "the optimal program" is meant to accomplish in the economy. They are instrumental in their nature and must be subject to permanent reevaluation in light of imposed patterns of economic development (Bromley, Schmid, and Lord 1971). The conflicting and complex nature of different objectives calls for a general model of project formulation and evaluation which will take into consideration the nature of individual projects and also plans or investment programs for the achievement of those developmental objectives.

Many choices are made which condition the economic feasibility of projects. As mentioned before, these choices are based on objectives articulated at the presidential, legislative, and ministerial levels. This implies that the economist/planner must consider the existing and potential relationships between the attributes attached to different projects and to the set of predefined goals and national priorities before the process of pure justification is carried out (Bromley and Beattie 1973).

A methodology is needed to help policy makers with these choices at different stages of the investment planning process. The methodology should respond to the specific questions which resolve the choice process at each level of decision making. The model presented in this book bridges this gap and helps the policy makers in choosing their investment program at their own level of aggregation. Before introducing the model, we present a very brief literature review.

McKean (1958) was one of the first to recognize the need to develop comprehensive models in the area of multiobjective evaluation (MOE). He offered a method that characterizes benefits of individual projects in monetary and nonmonetary terms. The relative desirability ("weights") or preference over these two types of benefits was for the policy maker to decide. These preferences were introduced into the analytics of BCA and some estimates of the worthiness would then help planners to choose the "best" group of projects. He saw the MOE problem as a question of measurability in the sense that all benefits and costs of individual projects could not be measurable in monetary terms.

Major (1969) offered an example of how to introduce MOE within the BCA context; his efforts were oriented to the modification of the ratios (discounted benefits over costs) which would enable the policy maker to obtain a more meaningful picture of the worth of each project. Instead of a simple BCA ratio he suggests a weighted average of different benefits and costs (national income as well as regional income); $\Sigma \alpha_i B_i / \Sigma \beta_i C_i$, where B_i and C_i represent benefits and costs, and α_i and β_i are different sets of weights. The limitations of Major's approach are (1) that he does not resolve the question of adequate mechanisms to determine the set of weights (the policy maker's role in selecting projects); (2) there is no explanation of the ways in which these ratios would "select" interrelated (complementary or substitute) projects; (3) his approach does not relate to the macro-economic targets and models developed which would help policy makers to know different programs' contributions to economic development; and (4) he focuses on individual projects, in toto, assuming that there are no budget limitations.

Other economists such as Marglin (1967) have assumed that the policy maker's behavior is characterized by a desire of maximizing one objective subject to the constraints of several others. In other words, a policy maker's preferences are made explicit through one objective, recognizing the boundaries of others.

Many economists have used a programming approach based on Major's philosophy of weighting objectives ($P = \Sigma \alpha_i f_i[x_i]$). One example of this approach was developed by McGaughey and Thorbecke (1972) who intended to relate this type of preference function to the area of macroeconomic targets by introducing indicators of a project's contribution to economic development. They used the ratio of benefits over costs, social productivity, output-investment ratio, labor-investment ratio, and foreign-exchange earning ratio. Their weighted ranking method, revealing the policy maker's objectives, was defined by a function that is represented mathematically as $R^P = yY^P + bB^P + eE^P$; where Y^P, B^P, and E^P are ordinal rankings of each project according to their separate contributions to income, employment, and foreign exchange, and y, b, e are the revealed weights of the policy maker.

Another group of economists has developed investment criteria reflecting the need for accomplishing a given type of macroeconomic impact and this approach is found in the work of Bruno (1972), Krueger (1972), Balassa and Schydlowsky (1972), and others. They are basically concerned with the policy maker's objective of achieving a certain balance-of-payments pattern, and they call this criterion "domestic resource cost" (DRC). They state that benefits and costs could be separated by their relations to the foreign and domestic sectors, and that these attributes are a priority within the policy maker's preference function; a recognition of the high cost of producing and saving one unit of foreign exchange.

Cohon and Marks (1973) have experimented with a two-objective model, and then they generalize the format for the n-objective situation. In the two-objective case, they define two main objectives: (1) national income (NI); and (2) environmental quality (EQ). Different types of project implementation will have different impacts on NI and EQ, respectively. These trade-offs are represented by a transformation curve in which NI is measured in money terms, and EQ in number of animals preserved. They call attention to the fact that, in simple one-objective maximization, efficiency through an optimum level of NI implies a specified level of EQ, the optimum level of NI is not necessarily that representing society's aggregate preferences. The optimum two-objective case is traced through the tangency between the transformation curve and society's welfare function.

The analytical model is generalized for an n-objective case through a multiobjective linear programming model. The main conclusion from the operational standpoint is that in a multiple objective problem we are not looking for a maximum maximorum; the main task is the definition of an efficient set of solutions (a noninferior set).

Keeney (1973) has developed a multiple-objective decision model in which there are six main steps to achieve the optimal solution: (1) define the real alternatives of the problem; (2) specify measures of effectiveness which will explicitly describe possible impacts on each important group concerned with the problem; (3) translate these measures of effectiveness of the different alternatives into relevant decision variables (cost, capacity, and so on); (4) identify each variable in terms of group impacts; (5) define the probability density function of the variables; and (6) define and maximuze a multiple-objective utility function. His main concern was to choose between different alternatives for a Mexican airport, given that the decision of improving airport facilities was already taken.

Candler and Boehlje (1971) have used a linear programming model for capital budgeting, given that a particular firm has multiple goals. One of the main problems is the reconciliation of different objectives with investment and price decisions. They state that the capital budgeting problem, with multiple objectives, can be expressed as an integer nonlinear programming problem. One of the conflict areas analyzed in the paper relates to the definition of the goal functions and the possible disagreement that can arise over the contribution of different investment alternatives to the goal functions. They suggest two possible solutions: expanding the number of goal functions, and accepting more than one scaling of goal function and running the capital budget for each scaling. The main conclusion of their paper relates to the effectiveness of capital budgeting involving multi-

ple goals, compared with those achieved in the one-objective procedure, in explaining the real investment priorities of the firm.

However, in spite of important contributions, none of these
models has served the purpose of bridging the gap between national
development planning and programming at the project level. They
have focused on individual projects and upon reduced form aggregation and limited objectives; they do not take into consideration the
relationship between investment strategies and the accomplishment
of predefined macroeconomic targets. In the next section we will
present a model which will help in the process of making investment
decisions within the development planning context of developing countries.

THE MODEL

The presentation of the model will be divided into two distinct
parts: investment selection and investment financing. These two
processes are not independent, and are only presented in this way
for simplification.

Investment Selection Model

Project and program formulators and evaluators, by applying
BCA on individual projects, compile a group of projects or investment proposals. At the same time, the CPO is providing policy
makers with the national, sectoral, and regional accounts projections,
particularly the macroeconomic targets which the optimal investment
bundle is expected to accomplish. Let us call them income $\bar{Y}$,
employment $\bar{E}$, and foreign exchange $\bar{F}$. Also, the CPO in concert
with the ministry of finance provides policy makers with the maximum
budget $(\bar{B})$ to finance these programs $(\bar{X})$.

The model provides a framework to allow the selection of the
optimal investment strategy based on their contribution (characteristics) to policy makers' social objectives $(\bar{Y}, \bar{E}, \bar{F})$. We call this
framework an investment-opportunity matrix whose rows group
different investment proposals, and whose columns list different
objectives or development targets (see Figure 2.2).

In recognition of budget limitations, the cost of these projects
cannot be greater than the available sources of funds (domestic and
foreign). The policy maker's objective function has been assumed
to be one of minimizing the difference between the investment proposal's contributions and the targets derived from the national
income models of the CPO. The policy maker wishes to minimize

FIGURE 2.2

Multiobjective-Hierarchical Investment
Decision Model

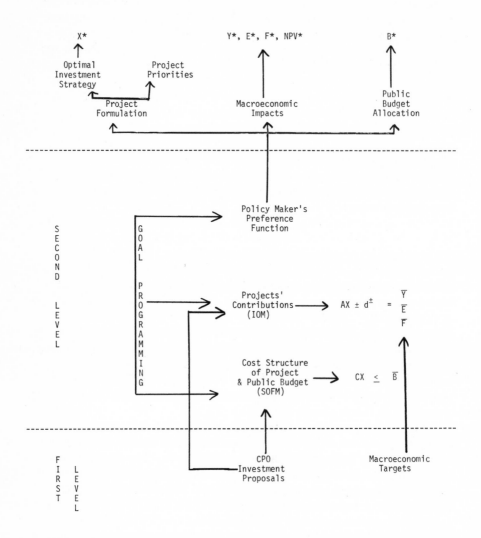

the deviations $(d_i^{\pm})$ between what projects contribute to economic development and the specified targets. This distance function will determine a "unique" solution (scalarization process) which contains the policy maker's preferences established in the vector of weights (α).

How does the planner, who supposedly will apply this model, determine the set of weights?* One situation might be characterized by the policy maker explicitly presenting the desired set of weights. In a situation in which no set of weights is revealed, the economist/planner is forced to undertake one of two possible courses of action. In the first, the economist subjectively determines the set of weights and, through sensitivity analysis—changing the appropriate values—assesses the basic trade-offs among different objectives. A second course of action sees the economist working interactively with the policy maker. The policy maker offers a tentative set of weights which, when introduced into the model, will determine the optimal investment bundle and the macroeconomic impacts. These results are presented to the policy maker who will review the output and suggest the new options which, by changes in the set of weights, will iterate to the desired solution.

The optimal value of the objective function—the distance function—is zero; exact accomplishment of society's objectives. Given the set of proposed projects; the government budget, the set of goals to be accomplished, the cost structure of projects, and the policy maker's preference function, we will use a goal programming (GP) model which we maintain is consistent with the policy maker's method of investment selection: minimizing the deviations between the projects' contributions and the prespecified set of multiple objectives. Some of the features of the model are presented in Figure 2.2.

Financial Model

In describing the cost structure of projects we have specified that investment selection is made in a context of limited financial resources, that is, capital rationing. Given the CPO estimates of foreign and domestic sources of funds, we can determine the optimal investment strategy for the economy (X^*). This strategy would be represented by the selection or ranking of a specific set of investments (X^*), their macroeconomic impacts (Y^*, E^*, F^*), the implied net present value of the program (NPV), and the optimal allocation of the government budget (B^*).

---

*The problem of weighting is also present in benefit-cost analysis at the first level in Figure 2.2.

FIGURE 2.3

The Economics of Project Financing

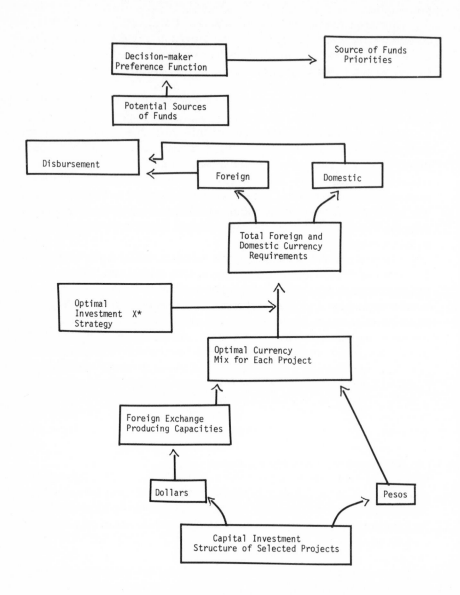

Source: Compiled by the authors.

However, the policy maker is confronted with the further problem of (1) allocating the budget (B^*) among different projects; (2) determining the requisite level of foreign funds to be borrowed; (3) determining the sources of these required funds; (4) determining the optimal mix, by project, of foreign and domestic funds; and (5) determining the optimal path and schedule for disbursing project funds. The analyses of these interrelated problems is presented in Chapter 6, with an overview presented in Figure 2.3.

SUMMARY

The investment decision model to be presented in detail in the following chapters is structured to be in accord with the basic nature of the decision process in most developing countries. It is intended to bridge the gap between a national plan based on specific macroeconomic targets and the selection of certain investment alternatives. The objective function is specified in terms of positive or negative deviations from a predetermined objective function defined with respect to the macroeconomic targets. The weights for the multiple aspects of the objective function can be determined in several ways. The final form of assistance is needed with respect to the economics of project financing. The increasing debt load of the developing countries makes it imperative that investment planning be cognizant of alternative sources of funds, alternative currency mixes by project, and optimal schedules for disbursing funds. The decision model developed here lends assistance in all of these important areas.

REFERENCES

Balassa, B., and D. M. Schydlowsky. 1972. "Domestic Resource Costs and Effective Protection Once Again." Journal of Political Economy 80 (January-February): 63-69.

Bromley, D. W., and B. R. Beattie. 1973. "On the Incongruity of Program Objectives and Project Evaluation: An Example from the Reclamation Program." American Journal of Agricultural Economics 55 (August): 472-76.

Bromley, D. W., A. A. Schmid, and W. B. Lord. 1971. Public Water Resource Project Planning and Evaluation: Impacts, Incidence, and Institutions. Madison: Center for Resource Policy Studies and Programs, University of Wisconsin, September.

Bruno, Michael. 1972. "Domestic Resource Cost and Effective Protection: Clarification and Synthesis." Journal of Political Economy 80 (January-February): 16-32.

Candler, Wilfred, and Michael Boehlje. 1971. "Use of Linear Programming in Capital Budgeting with Multiple Goals." American Journal of Agricultural Economics 53 (May): 325-30.

Ciriacy-Wantrup, S. V. 1971. "The Economics of Environmental Policy." Land Economics 47 (February): 36-45.

Cohon, Jared L., and David H. Marks. 1973. "Multiobjective Screening Models and Water Resource Investment." Water Resources Research 9 (August): 826-36.

Keeney, Ralph L. 1973. "A Decision Analysis with Multiple Objectives: The Mexico City Airport." The Bell Journal of Economic and Management Service 4, no. 11 (Spring): 101-17.

Krueger, Anne. 1972. "Evaluating Restrictionist Trade Regimes: Theory and Measurement." Journal of Political Economy 80 (January-February): 48-61.

Lancaster, Kelvin J. 1971. Consumer Demand: A New Approach. New York: Columbia University Press.

Major, David C. 1969. "Benefit-Cost Ratios for Projects in Multiple Objective Investment Programs." Water Resources Research 5 (December): 1174-78.

Marglin, Stephen. 1967. Public Investment Criteria. London and Cambridge, Mass.: George Allen and Unwin, and MIT Press.

Maslove, Allan M. 1976. "Public Sector Decision Making and the Technology of Consumption." Public Choice 27 (Fall).

McGaughey, Stephen E., and Erick Thorbecke. 1972. "Project Selection and Macroeconomic Objectives: A Methodology Applied to Peruvian Irrigation Projects." American Journal of Agricultural Economics 54 (February): 32-40.

McKean, Roland N. 1958. Efficiency in Government Through Systems Analysis. New York: John Wiley.

Sachs, Ignacy. 1970. "Selection of Techniques: Problems and
    Policies for Latin America." Economic Bulletin for Latin
    America 15, no. 1: 1-34.

Sandmo, Agnar. 1973. "Public Goods and the Technology of Con-
    sumption." Review of Economic Studies, October.

Steiss, A. W. 1972. Public Budgeting and Management. Lexington,
    Mass.: Lexington Books.

United Nations. 1972. "Conference of Human Environment."
    Development Digest 10, no. 2 (April): 3-4.

CHAPTER

3

**INVESTMENT CRITERIA
FOR CAPITAL
BUDGETING DECISIONS**

The purpose of this chapter is to present the basic elements of
project appraisal discussed during the early stages of capital budgeting developments. The essential characteristic of early capital
budgeting was to implement criteria and rules for project selection
on a project-by-project basis. The basic problem was to identify
sources and uses of capital which would permit the financing of
these individual projects.

A later state has been characterized by the use of programming
techniques, such as linear programming, to determine the optimal
allocation of limited funds to a set of investment projects. A section
of this chapter is devoted to the analysis of different models for
capital budgeting in the context of one objective. This section will
describe a series of concepts and transformations which will help
in understanding the features presented in the next chapter: capital
budgeting in a multiple objective context. One-objective optimization
models such as those of Lorie and Savage (1955), Weingartner (1963),
Baumol and Quandt (1965), and Carleton (1969) will be presented.
The first two models set the stage for most recent developments in
the area of capital rationing decision making.

BUDGETING INDIVIDUAL PROJECTS

The area of capital budgeting individual projects is primarily
associated with the writing of Joel Dean, with his work focusing on
two basic areas: project identification, and the specification and
measurement of the economic worth of proposed investments. For
Dean (1951, 1954) the capital budgeting process starts by identifying
the economic unit's anticipated needs for capital. The identification

24

of existing needs may be based upon (1) research about specific
activities and sectors of this economic unit—education, transportation, agriculture; (2) the necessity to reduce cost of particular
operations—import substitutions (foreign-exchange savings) or
introduction of cost-saving technologies; (3) development of new
areas of social demand—land reform or rural development settlement;
(4) recognition of basic economic linkages for the economic unit to
perform consequent activities—construction of highways; (5) stipula-
tion of "must" economic activity as a result of economic, social, or
political changes—nationalization and expansion of foreign companies;
(6) recognition of competition from other units in the economy,
foreign or domestic—export promotion; or (7) recognition of demands
on different products, activities, or programs—population growth
effects on education investments. The dynamics of the identification
process result in the creation of a "shelf of projects" which will
characterize and determine a specific structure of demand for capital.
Moreover, the analysis and developments of capital budgeting theory
must consider a complete assessment of the economic unit's supply
of capital; internal (domestic) or external (foreign).

The required stage in this process is the specification and
measurement of the economic worth of each of the proposed investments. Measurement of economic worth basically implies the
definition of a yardstick which will be applicable to all potential
investments. For Dean this yardstick must possess the following
characteristics. It

> should summarize in a single figure all the information
> that is relevant to the decision whether or not to make a
> particular investment, and none that is irrelevant. It
> should be applicable to all types of proposals and should
> permit appraisal in terms of a single set of standards . . .
> it should provide an index that is relatively simple to
> compute . . . finally, the yardstick should permit
> simple adjustments to allow for ranges of uncertainty
> in earnings estimates (Dean 1954, p. 123).

The yardstick that he proposed as a basic measure of economic
worth of investment projects was the productivity of capital. For
Dean, the ideal measure of capital productivity is given by that
interest rate which equates the present values of discounted cash
flows (benefits and operating costs) to the capital expenditures of
the project. The rate at which anticipated earnings equal the capital
cost of the activity is the internal rate of return (IRR). He compared
the IRR with other yardsticks such as the payback period and the
"degree of necessity" criterion. The payback yardstick is defined

as "the number of years required for the earnings on the project to pay back the original outlay with no allowance for capital wastage" (Dean 1954, p. 123). The degree of necessity, on the other hand, represents the degree of urgency of the proposed project (demand approach): "The extent to which it cannot be postponed to later years" (Dean 1954, p. 123). Under this characterization of the decision-making process—assessing the viability of individual projects—capital rationing is an activity which will provide planners with the "cut-off" IRR determined by the intersection of the supply and demand for capital. Once this cut-off rate is determined, the process not only considers the acceptance of projects but also this IRR represents a rejection rate. This rejection rate will tentatively assess the potential suitability of the overall economic unit's activities. Second, it will discriminate against low profitability projects. Finally, it supposedly implements long-run capital budgeting plans by, at the margin, eliminating low-productivity investments.

In the introductory description of the different investment criteria and rules,* two basic assumptions are made: (1) that all the costs and benefits associated with each of the investment activities are measurable, and that they are known with certainty; and (2) that capital rationing is absent (Henderson 1968, Hirshleifer 1970, and Baumol 1972). The second assumption will be considered particularly when comparison of the different criteria is made.

Some of the most popular criteria cited in the literature are as follows: net present value, internal rate of return, benefit-cost ratio, least cost, and payoff period. It is important to mention, prior to the conceptualization of these criteria, the distinction between a "criterion" and a "rule." Hirshleifer (1970, p. 48) makes this distinction an important part of his exposition stating that

> a criterion . . . is some mathematical formula (for example, present value) computed on the elements of a cost-benefit or payments stream. A rule indicates the acceptability of a project, by directing a comparison between the criterion computed and some other number or formula (for example, "adopt if the present value is greater than zero"). The failure to distinguish between rules and criteria has been responsible for considerable confusion, since in some cases divergent rules can be proposed for the employment of the same criterion.

---

*There are many other investment criteria that will not be presented here, such as Kahn (1951), Chenery (1953), and others. We will include the most traditional ones.

The present value of an investment is arrived at by discounting all prospective net benefits back to the present using a predetermined rate of interest. If there is no capital rationing, the correct course is to undertake all those projects which have a positive present value of discounted net benefits. The internal rate of return on an investment is that rate of interest for which the present value of discounted net benefits is zero. With this decision formula, and again on the assumption that there is no capital rationing, the correct course is to undertake all projects which have an internal rate of return higher than a predetermined rate of interest (Henderson 1968, p. 98).

The benefit-cost ratio (B/C) is a ratio between the present value of discounted net benefits to the present value of project costs. With this criterion, the decision maker will undertake projects with a B/C ratio greater than unity (the decision rule).

The least-cost criterion is arrived at by discounting back to the present the cost stream of a particular investment activity. Under a situation in which mutually exclusive projects exist, the least-cost rule tells the decision maker to take the project with the lowest discounted costs.

The payoff period (PP) is defined as that period that is required to accumulate positive benefits to cover the costs. This criterion can be used to rank projects in which the rule is to rank first the project with the smallest PP.

The internal rate of return criterion has the advantage, first, of being familiar to the financer and planners, since people are used to thinking in terms of rates of return on capital. Second, its calculation can be made without previous determination of the interest rate, on which there is much disagreement.*

There are also some limitations associated with the IRR. First, due to the calculations made in obtaining the IRR, there is possibly more than one value for the same project. This usually happens in investments in which the cost of abandoning an economic activity is high, or the financial compromises are assumed in future periods, or decreases in expected productivity of capital occur, or any other item that makes some future flows negative. Henderson (1968, p. 95) gives a possible solution for the problem when two rates are found in that they determine the interest rate feasibility interval.

Second, a serious limitation is encountered when formulation is concerned with sets of mutually exclusive projects. The rules applied based on this criterion for ranking will depend quite critically upon the level of the discount rate chosen.

----

*For instance, see Baumol (1968, 1969), Marglin (1963), Somers (1971), Feldstein (1964), and Masse (1962).

Third, under a capital rationing situation, because the marginal opportunity value of money in different periods must not be the same, the use of the IRR rule gives inconsistent results (Baumol 1972). This is an extremely important limitation in planning which deals, many times, with mutually exclusive projects.

Fourth, there are different concepts of IRR: average, marginal, and others, all of which confuse the applicability of the criterion. Henderson (1968) proves that, given a set of projects, the ranking outlay, using different conceptualizations of the IRR, is different. Moreover, as he points out, a project with high IRR is not, by definition, preferred to one with a lower IRR.

Fifth, the IRR criterion is calculated independently of the interest rate(s). Although the NPV accepts the possibility and is affected by different interest rates, the IRR does not. This represents a disadvantage which is associated with limitations in applying post-optimality analysis associated with a variety of interest rates.

Sixth, the implicit assumption that flows are reinvested at the IRR in the project is inaccurate. Mears and Siwijatmo (1974, p. 22) state that

> the most important is the implicit assumption that all net benefits, through either consumption or reinvestment, yield the same rate of return as the IRR, compounded through the remainder of the project's lifetime. This contradicts the assumption implied in the PV criterion that at the margin resources can bring consumption or reinvestment returns yielding only a rate of return equal to the social discount rate. This problem diminishes the more a project's benefits are realized towards the end of the project life.

If the IRR is significantly greater than the discount rate of interest, this criterion may overestimate the real profitability of the projects.

The payoff period criterion has been used in situations dealing with uncertainty. In certain types of projects characterized by a high degree of uncertainty to their benefits stream, a small payoff is very important. At the same time, this criterion, and the rule that goes with the use of it, is very weak because it does not take into account benefits which are far into the future.

The benefit–cost ratio can incorporate errors in the analysis of comparing projects: "In order to provide a result comparable with other criteria and with other projects evaluated by the same criterion, care must be taken to insure that benefits are shown 'gross' without first having been reduced by deduction of some of the costs. Changing quantities from the denominator to the numerator of a ratio will change the value of the ratio" (Mears and Siwijatmo 1974, p. 23).

The second limitation of the B/C ratio relates to the sensitivity of the ratio for changing the levels of benefits when current costs change. Mears and Siwijatmo (1974, p. 23) state that sensitivity "causes the criterion to discriminate against those projects with a large volume of output but a small per-unit profit margin as compared with those with a higher per-unit profit margin and small volume."*

The least-cost criterion is best when an economic state of mutually exclusive projects exists. This exclusivity is applied by discriminating against those projects with large net present value of costs. However, this criterion is very weak when reference must be made to the benefit side of projects, and when a minimum return to capital is expected.

Some of these comments have been conceptual in nature; others have been associated with practicing these rules. In our approach the net present value criterion will be applied because most of the shortcomings found in the other criteria are not present in the NPV. This is not to say that NPV does not have limitations. NPV is not sensitive to the size of the capital investment of different projects, or to other elements which are expressed in a reduced form (that is, different types of employment): "Its usefulness to rank alternative investments where capital budget constraints exist is limited to situations where two or more alternatives offer either (1) approximately the same present value of invested capital, or (2) approximately equal present value of annual benefits" (Mears and Siwijatmo 1974, p. 22).

The solution and the criteria proposed, and the explication of the relevant assumptions, set the basis for the major limitations of the project-by-project investment selection process. Among the major limitations to be mentioned—the ones which set the stage for another phase of development in capital budgeting theory—we will first note that this procedure places emphasis on the dynamics of budgeting on the physical investment side, with only a minor role for the financial process of investment selection and evaluation. Second, it does not precisely define the interrelationships and direct impacts of projects within the investment portfolio; they are independent of each other and supposedly achieve maximum profitability individually. Third, the criteria proposed focus on a unique objec-

---

*For an empirical application which manifests this weakness, see Mears and Siwijatmo (1974, Chapter 5).

tive such as economic efficiency.* Fourth, although great effort was made in defining the IRR concept, a series of questions was still unsolved such as the rate of reinvestment, or the implicit assumption that the economic unit would invest at a rate equivalent to the IRR. Finally, it was assumed that perfect certainty, perfect capital markets, and perfectly divisible investment alternatives exist.

CAPITAL BUDGETING AND MATHEMATICAL PROGRAMMING

Dean (1954), Heller (1951), Warren (1953), McLean (1958), Baldwin (1959),† and others have developed definite patterns to appraise investment projects. These include the conceptualization of a required yardstick as a screening device and as the only way to compare investments of different payback periods, economic life, and income streams. Moreover, they set the basis for future methodological development of investment theory by determining the major elements in cash flows and discounted values as they compare to other accounting concepts of suitability. Our major task in this section is to introduce a second stage of capital budgeting theory, mainly the evaluation of investment programs rather than isolated individual projects. For this purpose we will present the "Lorie-Savage problem" which contains three basic questions to be answered by capital budgeting theorists. Then we will present in detail the first programming approach to capital budgeting, the Weingartner method. Finally, some developments in the programming approach with special emphasis on the Baumol-Quandt model will be presented. These three pieces of work and some of their extensions represent the basic methodology of modern capital budgeting theory and will be explained in detail.

The Lorie-Savage Problem

Lorie and Savage (1955, pp. 229-39), in reformulating and criticizing Dean's approach, stated that an economic unit's investment decision-making process deals with three essential problems: (1)

———

*Dean (1954) did recognize that the firm has a variety of goals but no methodology was developed at that stage.

†See McLean (1958) and Baldwin (1959). In the McLean article interesting insights are developed to justify IRR as opposed to the payback criterion.

given the cost of capital, which group of independent investment should be accepted; (2) under conditions of capital rationing, what investment bundle should be undertaken; and (3) how to select optimally from among a set of mutually exclusive projects. To answer the first question they favor the calculation of the ratio between net present value of projects' cash flows and their cost; the latter which may be determined once the cost of capital is well defined. Even though it is an apparently simple criterion, they recognize some intrinsic difficulties. The basic difficulty appears when budget "discontinuities" are present. That is, when a project of considerable NPV absorbs all of the available budget under circumstances where two "small" projects (the capital cost of them is less than the former) generate a larger NPV.

The second major difficulty is created when there is a necessity to choose among projects with cash outlays in more than one period. The first approximation was to maximize NPV and exhaust the available budget in the first period, considering the possibility of having idle budget in the second or subsequent periods. However, many possibilities arise and a specific formula was developed which consisted of finding the optimal Lagrangian multipliers (p coefficients) p_1 and p_2 for those projects that have a positive $y - p_1c_1 - p_2c_2$; where y is the present value of the proposal, and c_1 and c_2 are the present values of the net outlay in the two periods, respectively. The p_1 and p_2 values are randomly chosen, respecting certain basic characteristics of the problem (limited budget). In particular, a pair (p_1, p_2) may result in none of the projects being approved (all $y - c_1p_1 - c_2p_2$ expressions are less than zero); or may result in all being approved but impossible to finance with the given budget. The rule then would be to find a pair of (p_1, p_2) in such a way that the budget is exhausted in both periods. The group of investments which comprise this bundle is the one which will maximize the "welfare" of the economy. If the problem considers three periods, the criteria to be considered is finding (p_1^*, p_2^*, p_3^*) for which $y - c_1p_1 - c_2p_2 - c_3p_3$ is greater than zero, and the budget is exhausted for the three periods.

Lorie and Savage illustrated this problem considering nine investment projects whose outlay and present values are described in Table 3.1. The available budget is 50 and 20 for each period. They started by assigning a (p_1, p_2) equal to (1, 3) which only resulted in a positive value of $y - c_1 - 3c_2$ for proposal d. By successive elimination of (p_1, p_2) pairs they determined that the optimal investment strategy contained projects a, c, d, f, and i which nearly exhausted the budget in both periods (48, 20). The basic principle behind this mechanism is to compare the capital rationing situation with one in which unlimited funds are available. In the latter situation, no shadow value is attached to the budget because, given that all investments have a positive NPV, there were sufficient funds to finance all of them. However, under conditions of capital rationing the sequential screening of projects depends upon the shadow price of one unit of capital (the p_1 and p_2). The ideal is to finance all of them; the nearer to budget exhaustion we are, the closer we are to maximum welfare.

As will be seen later, this approach has serious methodological limitations usually referred to as the "Hirshleifer paradox." As a practical matter, though, once the number of periods increases, the number or permutations required to find optimal values of the p's becomes unmanageable. Imagine for a moment the difficulty in finding the optimal values of a vector of p's $(p_1{}^*, p_2{}^*, \ldots, p_n{}^*)$.

For sets of mutually exclusive projects it was also suggested that the government select that project whose y - pc is the largest. When this project is identified, and should it require more financing than the available budget, changes in the optimal set of p's must follow, and all computations must be done again. This process, as mentioned before, also includes a combination of NPV and budget allocation adjusted by changing the values of p's which have already related to the cost of capital.

Lorie and Savage referred to the IRR criterion developed by Dean and assessed its limitations in comparison to their criterion. The Lorie-Savage criterion may be systematized in a simple mathematical form as follows:

Find $p^* > 0$ (j = 1, 2, . . . T) such that the expression $y_i - p_i c_i \geq 0$ for the projects being chosen. Here, T is the farthest time period, and $\sum\limits_{t=1}^{T} \sum\limits_{j=1}^{k} c_{ij} \leq C_t$ where C_t is the available budget in period t, and the expression $\dfrac{y_{k+1}}{c_{1,\,k+1}} \leq p_1 \leq \dfrac{y_k}{c_{1,\,k}}$ represents the condition for separation of the accepted to the rejected projects.

The Weingartner Model for
Capital Budgeting

To Weingartner, the Lorie-Savage procedure was incapable of adequately dealing with budget limitations in successive periods. "Their procedure, which is of a trial and error nature, does not guarantee a solution within a finite number of steps, nor will it work when there are substantial indivisibilities or interrelations in the investment alternatives being considered" (Weingartner 1963, pp. 3-4).

TABLE 3.1

Capital Outlay and NPV of
Alternative Investments

Investment	Outlay Period 1 (C_1)	Outlay Period 2 (C_2)	Present Value of Investment
a	$ 12	$ 3	$ 14
b	54	7	17
c	6	6	17
d	6	2	15
e	30	35	40
f	6	6	12
g	48	4	14
h	36	3	10
i	18	3	12

Source: James H. Lorie and Leonard J. Savage, "Three Problems in Rationing Capital," Journal of Business 28 (October 1955): 234.

His work represented the first attempt to introduce linear programming into capital rationing problems. As an introduction to the particular solution offered by Weingartner to the Lorie-Savage problem, we will first set the stage by analyzing two major sources of influence to Weingartner's work, and will then proceed to a full presentation of his model.

In a pioneering article, Henderson and Schlaifer (1954) presented the major informational advantages of mathematical programming for better decision making: the existence of limited resources for multiple uses, with all decisions being interlocked because of sharing a common set of fixed inputs. The major applications of linear programming they presented were to solve transportation problems, production, the combination of inputs and prices, and assessing low-cost production processes.*

In 1961 James C. Hetrick presented one of the first direct and practical applications of theoretical models to capital budgeting. The model was sought to determine what function capital was playing in an industry, its allocation, and the multiplicity of proper rates of return in various parts of the organization. He saw that the main function of capital was to allow management in developing activities that satisfy consumption of individuals in society. His budget allocation criteria may be summarized as follows:

> Suppose that management is considering one proposal to build Unit A and another to build Unit B, both in the same area of decision-making responsibility . . . the fact that the return for Unit A is higher than that for Unit B at all levels does not imply that all available capital should be invested in Unit A. Instead, the initial capital should go into Unit A until the point where the incremental return falls below the initial rate of return for Unit B. . . . At this point some funds should be diverted to Unit B in order to maximize the return to the enterprise as a whole (Hetrick 1961, p. 55).

In Dean's approach, allocation of the budget was subject to the IRR levels, while for Hetrick, measurement of IRR to each unit increase of the budget was to be calculated; the break-even point is determined by:

$$\frac{\Delta IRR^i}{\Delta C} = \frac{\Delta IRR^j}{\Delta C} \qquad\qquad (3.1)$$

where i and j are two projects. At equilibrium, the budget is exhausted at the point at which $\frac{\Delta IRR}{\Delta C}$ for all projects is equal at the last marginal unit allocated to each project.

The Model

Weingartner (1963) was the first to study the application of linear programming to the investment choice problem under condi-

---

*Another inspiring article for Weingartner's work was Charnes, Cooper, and Miller (1959) in which many applications of linear programming for the firm are presented. Also see Hirshleifer (1958).

tions of capital rationing. The presentation of his model will consider a proposed solution to the Lorie and Savage problem, the
duality implications, analysis of "fractional" projects, interdepend-
ency among projects, and the presentation of some major criticisms
to this approach.

The main problem to be solved is selection of the optimal investment strategy under conditions of capital rationing. With c_{tj} the
cost of individual projects, and c_t the budget constraint in period t,
b_j the present value of revenue and cost of project j, and X_j the
fraction of project j undertaken, the Lorie-Savage problem may be
solved by the following linear programming model:

$$\text{Maximize } \sum_{j=1}^{n} b_j X_j \qquad (j = 1, 2, \ldots, n) \qquad (3.2)$$

$$\text{Subject to } \sum_{j=1}^{n} c_{tj} X_j \leq C_t \qquad (3.3)$$

$$0 \leq X_j \leq 1. \qquad (3.4)$$

The objective function is determined by calculating, for each investment project, the net present value of benefits and costs. In particular, b_j represents a compound variable that may be defined as
$\sum_t B_{jt}/(1 + i)^t$, where 1 is the discount factor. For a given rate of
discount i in period t, B_{jt} is the expected net benefits of project i
in period t. The objective function then might be written as max
$\sum_{t=1}^{t} \sum_{j=1}^{n} B_{jt} X_j (1 + i)^t$. The decision variable X_j may be defined
as that fraction of the project that should be implemented if perfect
divisibility of the project is possible, or as the total acceptance or
rejection of projects (an integer variable in the interval 0, 1) if
indivisibilities are present. If the decision variables are defined
in fractional terms, the cash flows and the budget finally allocated
are proportional to the percentage each individual project is to be
implemented. Finally, due to the way in which this primal has been
stated, there is an implicit assumption that the projects are
independent—the acceptance or rejection of any of them will not
change the b_j values.

The constraints in this model are of two types: (1) budget or
available resources, and (2) constraints that define the domain of
X_j. The budget is assumed to have a fixed ceiling in each period,

and the constraints establish that the capital cost of each project must not exceed the budget. As for the second set of constraints, they will determine the bounds for the values of the X_j. When projects are divisible, X_j may take values between 0 and 1, while when projects are indivisible, X_j is constrained to a 0, 1 value. A special case is represented by a decision to rank the X_j's, which introduces a constraint where the sum of all X_j's must add up to 1 ($\Sigma X_j = 1$).

The Lorie–Savage problem presented in Table 3.1 might be solved by the following linear programming (LP) problem:

$$\text{Maximize } Z = 14X_1 + 17X_2 + 17X_3 + 15X_4 + 40X_5 +$$
$$12X_6 + 14X_7 + 10X_8 + 12X_9 \qquad (3.5)$$

Subject to

$$\begin{bmatrix} 12 & 54 & 6 & 6 & 30 & 6 & 48 & 36 & 18 \\ 3 & 7 & 6 & 2 & 35 & 6 & 4 & 3 & 3 \end{bmatrix} \begin{vmatrix} X_1 \\ X_2 \\ X_3 \\ X_4 \\ X_5 \\ X_6 \\ X_7 \\ X_8 \\ X_9 \end{vmatrix} = \begin{bmatrix} 50 \\ 20 \end{bmatrix} \qquad (3.6)$$

$0 \leqslant X_1, X_2, X_3, X_4, X_5, X_6, X_7, X_8, X_9 \leq 1$ whose solution is $X_1 = 1$, $X_2 = 0$, $X_3 = 1$, $X_4 = 1$, $X_5 = 0$, $X_6 = .97$, $X_7 = .045$, $X_8 = 0$, and $X_9 = 1$. That is, projects X_1, X_3, X_4, and X_9 should be fully implemented; projects X_2, X_5, and X_8 should be rejected, and X_6, X_7, should be implemented at a 97 percent and 4.5 percent level, respectively. This is practically the same solution proposed by Lorie and Savage.

By allowing for fractional projects in this particular case ($X_6 = .97$, $X_7 = .045$) the budget is completely exahusted. This is equivalent to the Lorie-Savage solution only if total acceptance or rejection of projects is permitted. The primal problem presented here has a corresponding dual which can be characterized as follows:

$$\text{Minimize } \sum_{t=1}^{T} \rho_t c_t + \sum_{j=1}^{n} \mu_j \qquad (3.7)$$

$$\text{Subject to } \sum_{t=1}^{T} \rho t^c_{tj} + \mu_j \geqslant b_j \qquad j = 1, 2, \ldots, n \qquad (3.8)$$
$$\rho t'_j \mu_t \geqslant 0$$

where ρ_t represents the opportunity cost (shadow price) of the present value of an extra unit of money added to the available budget in period t. If the budget is fully utilized (or binding) in any period t, the corresponding ρ will be greater than zero. The value of ρ will depend upon the ability, in an optimality sense, to fully utilize the budget. Finally, μ_t is the shadow price associated with the restriction imposed upon different values of the X's.

ρ_j and μ_j are part of the dual constraint $\Sigma \rho_j c_{tj} + \mu_j \geqslant b_j$. As before, b_j is defined as $\sum_t B_{jt}/(1+i)^t$–the present value of net benefits, and c_{tj} is the outlay implied by project j in period t.

Then $\mu_j \geqslant b_j - \sum_{t=1}^{t} \rho_t^* c_{tj}$; or to say that when a project is accepted,

$X_j > 0$ implies that we have an equality, which means that the social value of a project is equivalent to the excess of its present value over the discounted value of its outlays discounted at the opportunity cost ρ. For the rejected projects, given the slack variable $(\gamma_j) = 1 - X_j \geqslant 0$ or $X_j < 1$, it implies that $\mu_j = 0$ which incorporates γ_j^*, the difference between $\Sigma \rho_t c_{tj} + \mu_j^* - b_j$, where $\gamma_j^* = \Sigma \rho_j^* c_{tj} - b_j \geqslant 0$. By complementarity slackness γ_j^* will be equal to zero for fractional projects implying an optimization criteria that for any accepted project (even fractional) the present value of outlays must be equal to its net benefits, evaluated at the opportunity cost ρ, and the discount rate i, respectively.

The values of γ_j^* and μ_j^* are an output of the LP solution which Weingartner offered as a base for ranking projects; a ranking that may well differ from IRR or NPV rankings because it takes into account the projects' interrelationships via the budget constraint.

Consider the objective function–the relationship reflecting the minimization of the marginal profitability of available money resources–an objective which is congruent with the interpretation given to ρ_j^*. If ρ_j^* is positive, indicating that capital is the limiting factor in the corresponding period, then its marginal utility must be high. This function will minimize the total utility of all budget supplements available to the economic unit.

Fractional, Mutually Exclusive, and
Contingent Projects

Because allowance was made for the existence of fractional projects in this particular formulation, the budget was fully utilized. As a fundamental property of the model, there cannot be more fractional projects than the number of time periods considered. In a one-period problem, once projects are selected $(X_j = 1)$, the

budget that is left is more profitably invested in only one project
which will maximize the objective function of that supplemental
budget. In a two-period problem, only under rare circumstances
will one fractional project exhaust the budget left in both periods.
This implies that an extra fractional project will have to be introduced in the solution which will exhaust the budget in a "linear
combination" with the other fractional project. Let us analyze the
geometrical interpretation presented by Weingartner. In Figure
3.1, C_1 and C_2 represent the units of idle budget in periods 1 and 2,
respectively. The existence of one fractional project in a two-period
problem is represented by A^1 and a proportion of A^1 is required to
exhaust the available budget. But if A is to the right of A^1, the
budget in period 1 will be exhausted, with the difference $(\beta - \alpha)$ idle
in period 2. The full utilization of C_1 and C_2 will be accomplished
by finding a pair (α^1, β^1) which will finance α^1 of project A and β^1
of project B and which will exhaust the idle budget in both periods.
As observed in Figure 3.1, a third project is not feasible. Also,
project A will utilize $C_1 A$ and $C_2 A$ units in each period while project
B will utilize $\overline{C}_1 - C_1 A$ and $\overline{C}_2 - C_2 A$ in each period, respectively.

The introduction of mutually exclusive and contingent projects
does not present difficulties in a programming framework. For
mutually exclusive projects an extra constraint must be added:
$\sum_{j \epsilon J} X_j \leq 1$, j being the mutually exclusive project. This constraint
makes redundant the individual X_j's constraints for these X_j's ϵ J.
The presence of contingent projects is introduced by adding the constraint $X_r \leq X_s \leq 1$. Most interdependencies are treated by adding
complementary restrictions.

Because our major interest is with models for public budgeting,
we will not proceed with the Weingartner model and its extensions.
By way of shortcomings, several aspects warrant discussion. First,
the basic model does not consider the possibility of self-financing
by introducing an intertemporal function which would delineate the
ratio between consumption and investment—the saving function of the
model. Second, the objective function formulation contains a built-in
circular argument; the actualization of cash flows (b_j) is made by
introducing an exogenously determined discount rate, while the opportunity cost of capital is given by the dual (ρ^*). That is, for the
establishment of the objective function for the primal it is necessary
to have solved the dual. This has been called the Hirshleifer paradox.

The Baumol-Quandt and Carleton Reformulations

Baumol and Quandt (1965) criticized the Weingartner model on
two grounds: (1) restrictions imposed by the type of budget function;

FIGURE 3.1

Fractional Projects and Budget Utilization

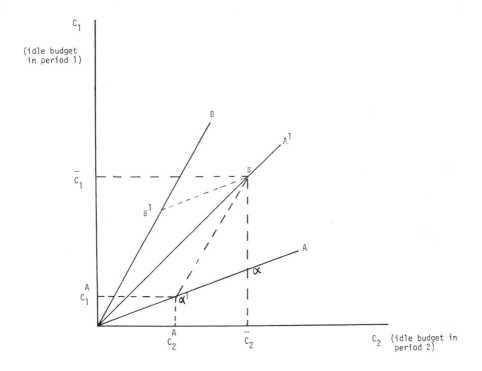

Source: Compiled by the authors.

and (2) the "appropriate" discount rate. They listed three problems
with the type of budget function: (1) the firm may invest or consume
with available funds; (2) funds idle in any given period may be retained
for later periods; and (3) the b_{jt} are not independent of the C_{jt}; these
requirements may be easily introduced by characterizing a saving
function, and intra/inter budget transfers. A more fundamental
problem of the Weingartner model is the discount rate. First, the
discount rate will be constant ($i_0 = i_1 = i_2 = \ldots = i_T$) if and only
if the economic unit is facing a completely elastic demand for capital:
it can borrow an unlimited amount of funds. Baumol and Quandt,
based on Fisher's theory of interest, offered an approach which argues
that in the absence of an external discounting procedure, the appropriate discount rate must reflect the social time preferences or
utility function of the economic unit and this is a subjective factor.
Their construct also encountered the Hirshleifer problem. To break

the circular argument of discount factors and opportunity cost of capital, Baumol and Quandt stated that the ultimate value of the selected investment strategy was the purchasing power over consumption generated. The major assumption in their model was that utility is a linear function of money.

If withdrawals in period t are designated by W_t, potential consumption expenditures, the model might be stated as follows:

Max $$\sum_t U_t W_t \qquad (3.9)$$

Subject to $$W_t - \sum_j b_{jt} X_j \leq C_t \qquad (3.10)$$

$$\rho_t \geq U_t$$

Which implies that $\frac{U_t}{U_{t'}} = \frac{\rho_t}{\rho_{t'}}$; the "marginal rate of substitution between withdrawals in the two periods equals the discount rate at the optimum if funds are withdrawn during both periods t and period t'" (Baumol and Quandt 1965, p. 326).

Carleton (1969) stated that both the Weingartner and Baumol-Quandt models are limited in three respects: (1) in neither model is the choice of objective function satisfactory; (2) neither rationalizes the routes of capital budgeting problems; and (3) they do not intrinsically relate capital budgets with the discount rate problem. For Carleton, the choice of a given investment package is functionally dependent upon the budgeting process and upon the redistribution process of the value added generated by such a package. His major reinterpretation is the inclusion of a distribution factor in the Baumol-Quandt model.

SUMMARY

The intent of this chapter has been to make the reader familiar with efficiency criteria for selecting individual projects and the application of linear programming to capital budgeting problems. Some of the efficiency criteria described here are the pay-off period, net present value, internal rate of return, and least cost. Some of the most controversial in the literature have been the pay-off period, net present value, and the internal rate of return. In the third section of this chapter we introduced the initial development of capital budgeting theory and the use of mathematical programming. Two major breakthroughs in the literature were marked by the Lorie-Savage model and the linear programming interpretation given by Weingartner. The Weingartner model was presented in detail with the explanation of the primal and dual problems, decision variables, shadow prices and their implications. The concepts presented here still apply for Chapter 4 and a clear understanding of this issue is necessary before proceeding. This model represents the foundation of modern capital budgeting theory.

REFERENCES

Baldwin, Robert H. 1959. "How to Assess Investment Proposals." Harvard Business Review, May-June, pp. 98-104.

Baumol, William J. 1968. "On the Social Rate of Discount." American Economic Review 58 (September).

_____. 1972. Economic Theory and Operation Analysis. 3d ed. Englewood Cliffs, N.J.: Prentice-Hall.

Baumol, W. J. et al. 1969. "On the Social Rate of Discount, Comments and Comments on the Comments." American Economic Review 59 (December).

Baumol, William J., and Richard E. Quandt. 1965. "Investment and Discount Rates Under Capital Rationing: A Programming Approach." Economic Journal 75 (June).

Carleton, Willard T. 1969. "Linear Programming and Capital Budgeting Models: A New Interpretation." Journal of Finance 24 (December): 825-33.

Charnes, A., W. W. Cooper, and M. H. Miller. 1959. "Application of Linear Programming to Financial Budgeting and the Costing of Funds." Journal of Business 32 (January): 20-46.

Chenery, Hollis B. 1953. "The Application of Investment Criteria." Quarterly Journal of Economics, February, pp. 76-96.

Dean, Joel. 1951. Capital Budgeting. New York: Columbia University Press.

_____. 1954. "Measuring the Productivity of Capital." Harvard Business Review, January-February, pp. 76-96.

Feldstein, M. S. 1964. "The Social Time Preference Discount Rate in Cost Benefit Analysis." Economic Journal 74, no. 294, pp. 360-79.

Heller, W. Walter. 1951. "The Anatomy of Investment Decisions." Harvard Business Review, pp. 95-103.

Henderson, P. D. 1968. "Investment Criteria for Public Enterprise." In Public Enterprise, ed. Ralph Turvey. Baltimore: Penguin Modern Economics, pp. 86-168.

Henderson, A., and Robert Schlaifer. 1954. "Mathematical Programming." Harvard Business Review, May-June, pp. 73-100.

Hetrick, James C. 1961. "Mathematical Models in Capital Budgeting." Harvard Business Review, January-February, pp. 49-64.

Hirshleifer, J. 1958. "On the Theory of Optimal Investment Decisions." Journal of Political Economy 66 (August): 329-52.

_____. 1970. Investment, Interest and Capital. Englewood Cliffs, N.J.: Prentice-Hall.

Kahn, Alfred E. 1951. "Investment Criteria in Development Programs." Quarterly Journal of Economics, February, pp. 38-61.

Lorie, James H., and Leonard J. Savage. 1955. "Three Problems in Rationing Capital." Journal of Business 28 (October): 229-39.

Marglin, Stephen. 1963. "The Social Rate of Discount and the Optimal Rate of Investment." Quarterly Journal of Economics, February.

Masse, Pierre. 1962. Optimal Investment Decisions. Englewood Cliffs, N.J.: Prentice-Hall.

McLean, John G. 1958. "How to Evaluate New Capital Investments." Harvard Business Review, November-December, pp. 59-69.

Mears, Leon A., and J. B. Djarot Siwijatmo. 1974. "Project Evaluation." Indonesian Cases and Exercises. University of Indonesia.

Somers, Harold M. 1971. "On the Demise of the Social Discount Rate." Journal of Finance 26 (May): 565-83.

Warren, Robert A. 1953. "Formula Plan Investment." Harvard Business Review, March, pp. 57-69.

Weingartner, H. M. 1963. Mathematical Programming and the
    Analysis of Capital Budgeting Problems. Englewood Cliffs,
    N.J.: Prentice-Hall.

CHAPTER

4

MATHEMATICAL FORMULATION OF THE MODEL: VECTOR OPTIMIZATION AND GOAL PROGRAMMING

This chapter will be devoted to the mathematical formulation of the method explained in general terms in Chapter 2. This will be done by introducing and describing the following: multiple objective/multiple criteria optimization and goal programming, the proposed mathematical model for investment selection; conceptualization of the policy maker's objective or preference function; possible reformulations of the model to take into consideration some special characteristics of investment decisions; several options of decision making under uncertainty; "time" as an endogenous variable in the model; and finally, the utility approach to project selection.

MULTIOBJECTIVE OPTIMIZATION AND GOAL PROGRAMMING

Recent developments in systems analysis have focused on problems characterized by multiple objectives. Often these objectives are conflicting or noncommensurable. In economic evaluation, the traditional approach has been the maximization of a unique objective (efficiency) with other considerations, such as environmental quality or regional employment, belonging to a system of constraints. However, policy makers are placing greater importance on factors usually relegated to the category of constraints and the model presented here is designed to deal with this approach.

Definitions

All of the methodologies presented in this chapter belong to the general class of vector optimization models as opposed to one objective optimization. The general statement of the vector optimization problem is:

$$\text{Max } Z(x) = [Z(x)_1, Z_2(x), \ldots, Z_n(x)] \tag{4.1}$$

$$\text{Subject to } g(x) \leq 0 \quad i = 1, 2, \ldots, m \tag{4.2}$$

$$x_j \geq 0 \quad j = 1, 2, \ldots, q$$

where $Z(x)$ represents a multidimensional objective function whose components are functions of the decision variables (x's). These functions are not necessarily measured in the same units and the system of constraints is represented by $m - g(x)$ inequalities. The feasible region of this problem has two different characterizations: (1) a feasible region in decision space which considers all those x's such that they satisfy $g_i(x) \leq 0$; and (2) a feasible region mapped into functional space $Z(x)$ which is also multidimensional.

Vectors cannot be maximized (or minimized) due to their multidimensionality, and thus we introduce the concept of noninferiority within the feasible region. This represents the conceptualization of efficient points by defining partial orderings between any two vectors. In particular, a vector x* is said to be a noninferior solution to the system of equations 4.1 and 4.2 if there does not exist another vector x' such that $Z_i(x') \geq Z_i(x^*)$, $i = 1, 2, \ldots, n$; strict inequality holding for at least one i.

The concept of noninferiority has been widely used in economics in finding the Pareto-optimal points (contract curve) in which the improvement of one function necessarily implies deterioration in the other. It is clear then that the finding of the noninferior set does not single out the optimal solution. This is to say that a noninferior solution is not necessarily an optimal solution, but the optimal solution is always noninferior.

Optimization procedures—sometimes called scalarization—must be defined in order to find a unique solution in the noninferior set. Different methods have been offered which will allow the decision maker to select this solution as a reflection of preferences among the objectives. Once these trade-offs among different objectives have been specified, the analysis is extended to decision space from functional space; for a given solution in functional space, in the absence of a duality gap, there is a corresponding point in decision space—both determining the scalar value of the objective function.

The next section covers goal programming and other methods for finding the optimal solution for the formulation and evaluation of public investment programs. The other methods will be presented as potential transformations of the objective function of the GP problem.

An Example

Consider an example which may clarify some of the basic concepts presented above.* Assume that we have two objectives:

Min $\qquad f_1 = x_1$ $\hspace{4cm}$ (4.3)

Min $\qquad f_2 = 10 - x_1 - x_2$ $\hspace{3cm}$ (4.4)

Subject to $\quad 0 \leq x_1 \leq 5$ or $g_1 = x_1 - 5$ $\hspace{2cm}$ (4.5)

$$g_2 = -x_1 \leq 0$$

$$0 \leq x_2 \leq 5 \text{ or } g_3 = x_2 - 5 \hspace{2cm} (4.6)$$

$$g_4 = -x_2 \leq 0$$

The first feature of this problem is that we are working in two spaces simultaneously: the space which bounds the feasible values of x's and the functional space which bounds the value of the vectoral objective function $F(x) = F\,(f_1[x],\ f_2[x])$. These two feasible sets are presented in Figure 4.1.

In general, there is no unique optimal solution in this problem; the minimum value of $f_1 = 0$ for $x_1 = 0$, while the minimum of $f_2 = 0$ occurs at $x_1 = x_2 = 5$ (which cannot be attained simultaneously). This implies the definition of a noninferior set (or a Pareto set) represented in this case by AB in Figure 4.1B. Additional criteria must be introduced—transformations in the objective functions—to reach one optimal solution; a preferred noninferior solution. The methodology used in this book to find the preferred solution is called goal programming.

As an introduction to the next section, the following discussion is a comparison of the basic features of goal programming and linear programming for capital budgeting. Goal programming differs from linear programming in several important respects. First, it enables a decision maker to deal with the nonexistence of a common, feasible set of solutions by revealing a satisficing solution. That is, given a set of goals and constraints, GP will yield a combination of preferred investment activities and will specify the degree to which the goals have been accomplished. This is of singular importance in the context of developing countries, since few governments are seeking the optimum optimorum, but rather are seeking to determine how far society is from a set of prespecified goals.

---

*This example is taken from Haimes, Hall, and Freedman (1975).

FIGURE 4.1

Decision and Functional Space

(a) Decision Space

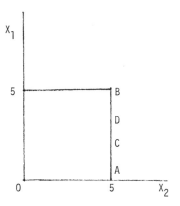

(b) Functional Space

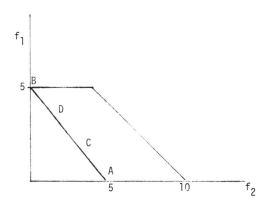

Source: Compiled by the authors.

The objective of goal programming is not the maximization or minimization of a single objective criterion. Instead, the objective is to attain a certain set of goals, which are rated by priority factors, as closely as possible; the procedure we will follow is the minimization of deviation between the goal and what we can achieve within the given decision environment (Lee 1972).

Goal programming, then, minimizes a multidimensional objective function that contains the relevant deviations from all of the goals of each of the investment activities considered by the government in its development planning (Hawkins and Adams 1974). Moreover, a distinctive feature which sets goal programming apart from the simplex method of linear programming is the fact that instead of maximizing or minimizing a given type of objective criterion directly, GP minimizes the deviations between preestablished goals and what the projects (means) actually achieve within the given set of constraints. Slack variables in the simplex method are used as dummy variables rather than being the principal component of the objective criterion (Lee 1971). Positive and negative deviations from the goals produce information regarding which goals are underachieved, which are overachieved, and the extent of this deviation.

The admissability of multiple conflicting goals gives government planners the possibility of ranking goals via the a priori assignment of weights. This hierarchy of goals will have two principal effects: high-level goals will be satisfied before low-level goals, and planners have the opportunity to review and revise, over time, the set of priorities in light of specific solutions derived from the model.

The ranking of goals is done by attaching weights to the multiple deviational variables within the objective function. This method, which is the most flexible property of GP, will allow the decision maker to weight differently overachievement and underachievement of different goals. For example, if the government wants to generate $1 million of net national income and specifies that underachievement of this goal matters more than overachievement, GP will solve it by an appropriate transformation of the objective function. This feature gives this model a greater flexibility when applied to public decisions where the quantitative and qualitative nature of over- and underachievement are very different.

Another difference between linear programming and goal programming is that no transformation of the objective function is needed in the latter when incorporating constraints that are measured in the same units.

THE MODEL

By way of introducing the model, assume that at the end of the investment selection process a set of investments is presented to the policy makers, call them X_1, X_2, . . . , X_n. At the same time, the policy maker has stated that the main goals of the economy are G_1, G_2, . . . , G_m. The economist/planner prepares the investment opportunity matrix by determining the contribution of each X_i to each G_j; call them A_1, A_2, . . . , A_m. In particular, A_j is a vector whose characteristic component is an element a_{ij}, that is, the contribution of project X_i to goal j.

The goal vector (G)—or the macroeconomic targets to be accomplished by the government investment program—is defined by the Central Planning Office based on national and sectoral account models. This vector is an expression of what the economy should accomplish within the preestablished planning period; say, create 20,000 new jobs, generate \$100 million of new regional income, and generate \$20 million in foreign exchange. The model also provides assistance to policy makers even under circumstances where these values might not be available. Here, it is only necessary to state the direction of preferences; "the more jobs the better." This type of statement needs little or no transformation for its incorporation in this model. Using the employment example, we would transform each a_{ij}, where j refers to employment, for every project X_i into $1/a_{ij}$ and a corresponding $G_j = 0$.*

The set of projects might over-, under-, or exactly accomplish a specific goal. This phenomenon is specified in the model by introducing "deviational variables" (d_i^+, d_i^-) to measure the levels of goal accomplishment. They will also be the main variables in the objective function of the model. In particular, if there is an overaccomplishment of a specific goal, its d^+ will be greater than zero, and the appropriate d^- will be equal to zero. By the same token, if there is underaccomplishment ("slack"), d^- will be greater than zero with d^+ equal to zero. This general property of the d^+s and d^-s is called "orthogonality" and can be introduced as an equation of the model: $d^+ \times d^- = 0$.

A characteristic mathematical representation of our set of goals in the GP model is

$$\Sigma \ AX - Id^+ + Id^- = G \qquad\qquad (4.7)$$

for each project i, each goal j, and each period t.

Two sets of optional constraints used in this model deserve specific attention. One set is the equation representing the budget; we have the cost structure of each project in each time period (call it C_i), and the available budget in each period (B^t). The mathematical formulation is:

$$CX \leq B \qquad\qquad (4.8)$$

The second set of equations refers to the values of X's. We present two options: one will tell the policy maker the optimal

----

*As will be seen in Chapter 6, this type of transformation in the model can be used to rank different foreign sources of funds.

financing level of each project, and the other will tell the policy
maker the ranking or project priorities. The first one is mathematically represented by the following inequality:

$$0 \leq x \leq 1 \qquad \text{or } X = \begin{cases} 0 \\ 1 \end{cases} \qquad (4.9)$$

(divisible   (indivisible
 projects)   projects)

and the second by

$$\Sigma x = 1 \qquad (4.10)$$

Other constraints representing mutually exclusive projects, subordinate projects, sequential projects, and the like may also be
introduced.

The last equation that must be explained is the objective function
of the model: that which represents the policy maker's preferences.
Here we assume that it is to minimize deviations between the contributions from the investments and the established objectives. This is
mathematically represented by

$$\text{Min } D = \alpha \left| \Sigma Ax - G \right| \qquad \text{or} \qquad (4.11)$$

$$\text{Min } D = \Sigma \alpha_i^+ d_i^+ + \alpha_i^- d_i^- \qquad (4.12)$$

where $d_i^{\pm}$ are the deviational variables and the α_i represent the policy
maker's priorities—the set of weights.* This objective function may
be transformed to answer different sets of questions, some of them
presented in a later chapter.

A full expression of the model may be represented by

$$\text{Min } D = \Sigma \alpha_i^+ d_i^+ + \alpha_i^- d_i^- \qquad (4.13)$$

Subject to

$$Ax - Id^+ + Id^- = G \qquad (4.14)$$

$$0 \leq x \leq 1 \quad \text{or } \Sigma x = 1 \quad \text{or } x = \begin{cases} 0 \\ 1 \end{cases} \qquad (4.15)$$

$$d_i^+ d_i^- = 0 \qquad (4.16)$$

$$x, d_i^+, d_i^- \geq 0 \qquad (4.17)$$

---

*The absolute value of the difference is only one way of repre-
senting a distance function. More details are found in a later section
of this chapter. A general representation may be written as follows:

The implementation of this model considers three major outcomes: project selection; macroeconomic impacts, and, by residual, government budget allocation. Project selection in a multiobjective framework is achieved by determining a "satisficing" solution for the x_i (projects). In cases of project divisibility, the model will determine the optimal proportion up to which a project should be financed ($x_1 = .50$, $x_2 = 1.0$, . . . , $x_n = 0$). If project indivisibilities are present, 0 or 1 values may be attached to the decision variables providing a "go-no go" signal—total acceptance or rejection of projects. Finally, the goal programming methodology will also enable planners to set preferences through project priorities by the determination of a preference vector, $\Sigma x_i = 1$.

The optimal investment strategy, or the optimal structure of the capital stock in the economy, is determined by the model under the following assumptions: that the investment bundle is large relative to national income, that there are project interrelationships, and that there exists a very inelastic supply of capital.

The second feature of this model is that it generates the expected potential flows of selected economic indicators for each possible investment strategy under consideration. The model provides this information by adding (or subtracting) to the vector of prespecified goals the deviational variables ($d_i^{\pm}$)—also part of the decision variable vector—that, in this case, indicate the levels of over- and under-accomplishment of different goals. The capacity to state these flows permits us to have knowledge of the extent of the major trade-offs (whenever they are present) derived from a given set of expenditure policies. Each investment bundle will impose a unique pattern of economic development.

Assume that a particular production process may be expressed in a GP framework as follows (Lee 1972):

Min:
$$Z = P_1 d_1^- + P_2 d_4^+ + 5P_3 d_2^- + 3P_3 d_3^- + P_4 d_1^+ \qquad (4.18)$$

Subject to:
$$x_1 + x_2 + d_1^- - d_1^+ = 80 \qquad (4.19)$$

$$x_1 + d_2^- = 70 \qquad (4.20)$$

$$x_2 + d_3^- = 45 \qquad (4.21)$$

$$x_1 + x_2 + d_4^- + d_4^+ = 90 \qquad (4.22)$$

$$x_1, x_2, d_1^- \geq 0 \qquad (4.23)$$

Min $D = || \underline{f}(\bar{x}) - \hat{\underline{f}} ||$ where $|| \times ||$ denotes any norm, $\underline{f}(\underline{x})$ is a vector of objective functions, and $\hat{\underline{f}}$ is the policy maker's vector of goals.

where P_i's represent attached weights to the positive or negative deviations from the goals ($d_i^{\mp}$'s); equation 4.19 represents capacity; equation 4.20 represents minimum sales of product x_1; equation 4.21 represents minimum sales of product x_2; and equation 4.22 represents a constraint on the maximum utilization of overtime (that is, excess capacity).

Figure 4.2A describes the feasible region of this problem. If the problem is to minimize the underutilization of the actual capacity, Figure 4.2B represents its feasible region. However, if, at the same time, there must be a minimization of the overtime, Figure 4.2C represents the overall feasible region.

A linear programming problem which achieves the same optimal solution may be represented by

$$\text{Max: } 2,500x_1 + 1,500x_2 \tag{4.24}$$

$$x_1 \leq 70 \tag{4.25}$$

$$x_2 \leq 45 \tag{4.26}$$

$$x_1 + x_2 \leq 90 \tag{4.27}$$

$$x_1, x_2 \geq 0 \tag{4.28}$$

The comparison of system of equations 4.18–4.23 and system of equations 4.24–4.28 seems to suggest that the linear programming and goal programming solutions would yield the same answer if conversion of goals into constraints is allowed. However, this is not the case. Assume, for example, that the constraints set by certain goals do not form a convex set of feasible solutions–see, for example, the system of equations 4.29–4.32. In this case there is no solution using linear programming; but, because goal programming determines a satisficing solution, this problem may be solved by GP. To illustrate the case, consider the following example.

$$\text{Max: } 2,500x_1 + 1,500x_2 \tag{4.29}$$

$$x_1 \geq 100 \tag{4.30}$$

$$x_2 \leq 45 \tag{4.31}$$

$$x_1 + x_2 \leq 90 \tag{4.32}$$

It can be seen immediately that there is no convex feasible region (see Figure 4.2D). However, if the GP method is applied, there is a clear solution to the problem, which will introduce deviational

FIGURE 4.2

The Graphic Solution of Goal Programming

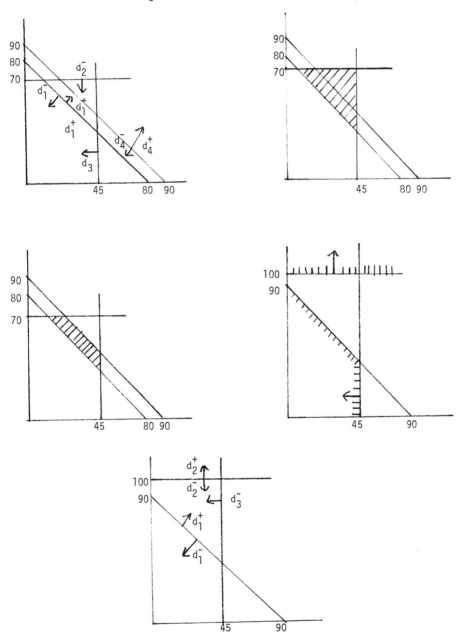

53

variables to allow over- and underachievements of the specified goals (see Figure 4.2E).

POLICY MAKER'S OBJECTIVES: THE CHOICE OF A DISTANCE FUNCTION

So far we have represented our policy maker's preferences as a set of characteristic values, or merit-want parameters, that are statistically expressed by numerical targets and their deviational variables. There are many ways of representing these distances, and this section is concerned with the concept of a distance function and the transformations resulting from the introduction of deviational variables in the set of equations representing the policy maker's objectives.

The absolute value of the difference between Ax (means) and the vector b (goals) represents only one way to express a distance function. The main topological characteristics of a distance function might be expressed as follows (Nikaido 1972):

(a) $d(Ax, b) \geq 0$
(b) $d(Ax, b) = 0$ if and only if $Ax = b$
(c) $d(Ax, b) = d(b, Ax)$
(d) $d(Ax, b) \leq d(Ax, z) + d(z, b)$ (the "triangle inequality")
(e) If $Ax \neq b$, then $d(Ax, b) > 0$

Distance functions that fulfill the axioms which may be used in this type of decision model are, for example, the one represented by the expression $\Sigma [(Ax - b)^2]^{\frac{1}{2}}$, which can be generalized by defining the expression $[\sum_{i} (Ax - b)^\eta]^{1/\eta}$ where the hierarchy imposed by the objectives will determine the lexicographic procedure for solution (see next section).

In a more abstract way we may also represent distance functions, which differ from the one just stated in the way the model converges to a solution. In particular, consider two other definitions of distance between real numbers and compare their method of convergency. For example, $d_1(Ax, b) = \sqrt{(Ax\ b)^2}$ and $d_3(Ax, b) = \text{Max} \, |(Ax - b)|$ are other types of distance functions. In two dimensions, assuming a normalization to 0-1 space, these distance convergencies are described graphically in Figure 4.3 A, B, and C, respectively.*

---

*In the case of points defined in two dimensions $p = (a_1, a_2)$ and $q = (b_1, b_2)$, $d_1(p, q) = \sqrt{(a_1 = b_1)^2 + (a_2 - b_2)^2}$, Figure 4.3B; $d_2(p, q) = |a_1 - b_1| + |a_2 - b_2|$, Figure 4.3A; and $d_3(p, q) = \text{Max} \, (|a_1 - b_1| + |a_2 - b_2|)$, Figure 4.3C.

FIGURE 4.3

Topological Convergency of Different Distance Functions, an Illustration in a Normalized Two-Dimensional Space: $X_1 \varepsilon\ [-1,\ 1]$; $X_2 \varepsilon\ [-1,\ 1]$

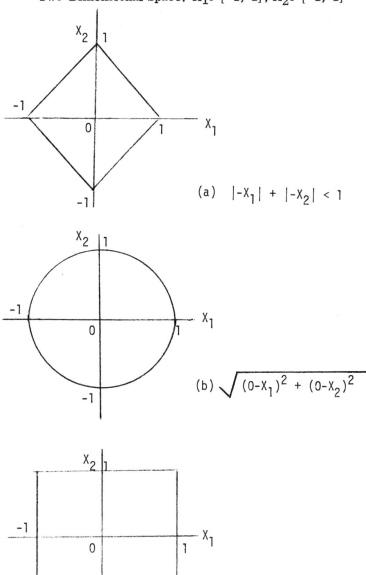

(a) $|-X_1| + |-X_2| < 1$

(b) $\sqrt{(0-X_1)^2 + (0-X_2)^2}$

(c) $(|0-X_1|\ ,\ |0-X_2|) < 1$

Source: Compiled by the authors.

There are many other forms of distance which do not violate the axioms stated above. It is important to note, though, that some forms of distance functions will violate the assumptions of linearity, in particular, $d_1(Ax, b)$.

The transformation of linear programming into a GP system has a very specific geometrical interpretation. Assume that the objective function in the LP problem is represented by $\Sigma a_i x_{ik} = S_k$. Define $u_k = \Sigma a_i x_{ik} - S_k$. The variable u_k may take either positive or negative values. To allow the existence of these values into the objective function of the GP problem, define $u_k = d_k^+ - d_k^-$, where the $d^{\mp}$'s are positive and negative deviations whose meaning is the same as stated before.

When describing the feasible region of the problem under consideration, the transformation of the variable u_k into two auxiliary variables—d_i^+ and d_i^-—explicitly introduces a new axis of real numbers. Figure 4.4A describes the feasible region for the cases of a variable u_k without transformation. If no transformation is allowed, this variable takes positive and negative values.

However, if u_k is transformed into the two auxiliary variables— d_i^+ and d_i^-—a new axis is introduced (see Figure 4.4B). Two new feasible points (F_1 and F_2) appear when the transformation of u_k is realized. In order to avoid solutions that take into consideration these new points, a method of solution which only considers extreme points has to be used. In using the GP model, the simplex method of solution which identifies a solution only at the extreme points is used.

CHARACTERISTICS OF DECISIONS AND MODELING OPTIONS

Depending upon the specific government decision, there are other forms which the objective function may take. If the main purpose of planners is to satisfy a high-priority objective to a specific level before other lower-priority objectives are satisfied, lexicographic programming is the most appropriate approach; if the decision maker must select those activities which generate the highest attainable level of each of the objectives, disjunctive programming is the most appropriate; and if the decision maker wants to accomplish the simultaneous set of goals to specify project levels and priorities, goal programming is the most appropriate. The first two approaches have not been discussed and will be explained briefly. Given that the economist/planner has identified the primary attributes of the investment activities under consideration, the basic mechanism behind the application of the lexicographic model is that of a hierarchy

FIGURE 4.4

Introduction of Deviational Variables:
A Geometric Interpretation

A. Original Convex Set

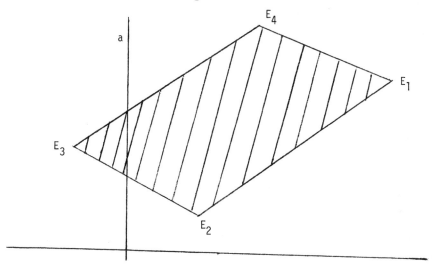

B. Transformed Convex Set

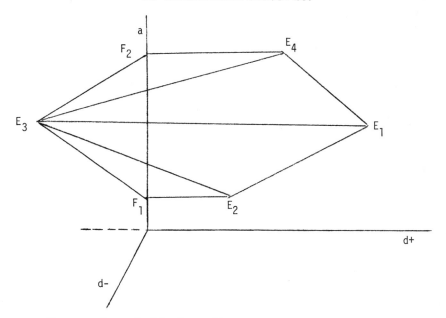

Source: Compiled by the authors.

of importance among those attributes. A decision maker may decide
between two alternatives based on the most important attribute
irrespective of the relative position in terms of other dimensions.
If the two alternatives are equally beneficial to the economy based
on the first attribute, the planner turns to the second most important
attribute, and so on.

The generalized form of lexicographic programming is

$$\text{Max: } D = D(d_1, d_2, \ldots, d_m)$$

Subject to: $Ax - 1d^+ + 1d^- = b; \ 0 \leq x \leq 1$

which reads: if and only if $d_1 \geq \bar{d}_1$, then max w_2

if and only if $d_2 \geq \bar{d}_2$, then max w_3

.   .

.   .

.   .

if and only if $d_{m-1} \geq \bar{d}_{m-1}$, then max w_m

where w_i symbolizes the welfare that is associated with the accomplishment of a variety of goals. The relation between all the goals
may be linear, and the arguments of each goal (x's) may also be
linear; but linearity is not necessary.

One of the problems associated with the partial application of
the lexicographic procedure is the accomplishment of transitivity
among preferences. If the definition of the model is not adequate,
it may generate intransitive preferences and, thus, contradictory
solutions.

Conjunctive and disjunctive procedures represent another method
that may be used in project formulation and selection when dealing
with multiple objectives. Dawes (1964) describes two main characterizations of this model: conjunctive selection procedures (CSP),
and disjunctive selection procedures (DSP). CSP is a process of
formulation and selection of investment opportunities by the evaluation of their least-relevant attribute. This procedure allows the
ranking of activities, or sequential elimination procedures, taking
into account that the objective is to eliminate the "worst" projects.
DSP is a process of project formulation and selection in which evaluation is made based on the project's greater contribution. This DSP
procedure has been widely used by governments. For example,
when the economy is facing serious problems of unskilled labor
unemployment, their typical response has been to improve labor
absorption by implementing housing construction, which utilizes
rather unskilled labor (see ILO [1972]).

The transformation of the objective function is simple and can be expressed in the CSP case as Min (a_{ij}), where a_{ij} represents attribute i. One of the typical applications of this objective function is to state a "minimum" accomplishment of some particular attribute in order for a project to be accepted. In the DSP procedure, the opposite method is followed: the transformation consists in Max (a_{ij}).

One of the important features of these two procedures is the possibility of using them simultaneously. They will set the upper and lower bounds for each of the attributes, which is particularly important when too many projects are in the potential feasible set and an easy discrimination, through the setting of the upper and lower bounds, is needed.

Searching for the dominant solution might also be a method of sequential elimination of investment activities during the process of formulation and selection (see Papandreou and Zohar [1974]). When the number of activities is large, this method generally does not result in an "optimal" solution. However, the concept of sequential elimination through the dominance procedure can also set the upper and lower bounds of the feasible set, with the purpose of eliminating the "worst" projects.

A parametric approach assumes that the decision maker knows the relative trade-offs among all the attributes under consideration. The preferred solution is found by

$$\text{Max} \sum_i \theta_i Z_i (x) \tag{4.33}$$

$$\text{Subject to } g_i (x) \leq 0 \tag{4.34}$$

$$x \geq 0 \sum_i \theta_i = 1$$

where θ_i represents a given set of weights.

This approach was first introduced by Major (1969) to reformulate the simple ratio of benefits to cost to reflect priorities at the national and regional levels. Changes in the set of parameters allowed him to determine the so-called benefit transformation curve (the noninferior set). One of the major limitations relates to the defined externalities among different objectives—a given level of $z_i(x)$ is a function of $z_j(x)$ levels. This requires not only the determination of a given θ_i for a stated level of $z_i(x)$, but for all levels of $z_i(x)$.

With the ε-constraint approach, the major difference with the general statement of GP is that the decision maker determines the "acceptable" level of objective functions bringing them into the constraints. The problem may be stated as follows:

Max $z_1(x)$ (4.35)

Subject to $z_i(x) \leq \varepsilon_i$ $i = 2, 3, \ldots, n$ (4.36)

$g_i(x) \leq 0$ (4.37)

$x > 0$

The surrogate worth trade-off method was first developed by
Haimes and Hall (1974) and represents an extension of the ε-constraint
approach. They demonstrated that the trade-off functions can be
found from the dual variables (Lagrangian multipliers) of the following
problem:

Max $z_1(x)$ (4.38)

Subject to $z_j(x) \leq \varepsilon_j$ $j = 2, 3, \ldots, n$ (4.39)

$g_k(x) \leq 0$ $k = 1, 2, 3, \ldots, m$ (4.40)

$\varepsilon_j = z_j(x) + \bar{\varepsilon}_j$

$\varepsilon_j \geq 0$

where $z_j(x)$ is the global minimum of the jth function; and ε_j is varied
parametrically to construct the trade-off function defined as $T_{ij}(x) = \dfrac{dz_i(x)}{dz_j(x)}$.

In the rest of this section we will illustrate how these possible
reformulations of the basic programming model can be of assistance
to decision makers. There might be some confusion as to when we
might use a disjunctive or conjunctive procedure or a lexicographic
procedure. Here, we will discuss situations in which different transformations of the proposed model can help policy makers in assessing
the basic trade-offs involved in their decisions.

We begin by describing a situation in which the model can be
directly applied. UNDP and IDB (UN Development Program and
Inter-American Development Bank) held a Mid-Project Evaluation
Workshop in June of 1975 to discuss the investment strategy and
planning methodology for irrigated agriculture in Latin America
(IDB/UNDP 1975). This project has three objectives: formulate
investment strategies for irrigated agriculture, establish a methodology for project design, and recommend evaluation procedures.
The socioeconomic perspectives of project design and evaluation—
independent of the existing microeconomic allocation of resources—
considers mainly the rapid increase of farmers' incomes, the
generation of employment, increased production efficiency, a

reduction in the balance-of-payments gap (food), and a move toward a more "proper" distribution of income. The goal programming approach is consistent with problems formulated in this way and would be relevant for helping countries to ascertain national irrigation strategies, determine the trade-offs among different objectives, and determine the level of goal accomplishment by the proposed strategy. Countries, as well as UNDP or IDB, might use the model to screen and determine the optimal investment strategy in the irrigation sector in Latin America based upon established macroeconomic targets (national or sectoral). This decision-making model can yield the real impacts of irrigation projects (in this case) on key social goals such as income (level and distribution), employment, regional growth, and balance of payments.

We have also discussed disjunctive and conjunctive models, lexicographic models, dominant solutions, interactive programming, and the like. We will describe two cases: one in which disjunctive and another in which lexicographic procedures might have been applied to help planners avoid undesirable outcomes. Disjunctive selective procedures would select projects based on their greater contribution or their "most" important attribute. However, the selection of projects in this "maximax" fashion may cause, under certain circumstances, very undesirable—even irreversible—trade-offs among different objectives in the economy. For instance, in 1970-71 the Chilean economy was suffering from high rates of unemployment and the government considered solving unemployment to be its highest priority objective. Policy makers distributed the government budget and then selected projects based on a specific disjunctive procedure: selecting those projects which had a large employment component. Priorities were given to the housing construction sector based on its employment demand composition, assuming that housing and building activities would employ around 50 percent more labor than any other infrastructural investment. This decision was implemented by a significant increase in the housing sector budget. This program created jobs in three ways: (1) increasing the budget (15,700 new jobs); (2) changes in the composition of government expenditures (3,900 new jobs); and (3) promoting special programs (30,000 new jobs). In total, the disjunctive nature of this decision created 49,600 new jobs in 1971, not counting those indirect jobs created because of the multiplier effects, or competitive labor use by the private sector. This extraordinarily high employment component of an investment strategy of this nature created increased income, but also increased aggregate demand (inflation) and inflicted serious pressures upon the balance of payments (increasing food imports) (ILO 1972). The model presented here would have been helpful to policy makers in determining the optimal level of government budget allocation which would have minimized adverse effects on other social objectives.

Finally, we would like to point out that there are many government decisions which might be characterized as lexicographic. One
of the most traditional and well known lexicographic procedures is
when policy makers design growth and development strategies over
time. A country might first need to accomplish a predetermined
income level, then, once this level is accomplished, policy makers
might want to close the balance-of-payments gap, and so on. This
model offers policy makers a consistent framework to select sequential development projects taking into consideration lexicographic
priorities of a particular government. Additionally, all of these
models may be used in a combined fashion depending upon the decision
and the complexity of the project selection procedures.

DEALING WITH UNCERTAINTY

Uncertainty in a goal programming problem is characterized by
defining the sources of uncertainty. Basically, uncertainty can be
associated with the vector of weights ($d_i^{\pm}$'s), elements in the investment opportunity matrix (a_{ij}'s), the source-of-funds coefficients,
the right-hand side or goal vector (b_i's), and other structural factors
that affect the behavior of the model, and, thus, the optimal solution.
There are methods for dealing with uncertainty which have already
been applied to linear programming problems, and they will be discussed briefly. Madansky (1962, pp. 463-64) states that

> most linear programming problems involve uncertainty
> in either the technology matrix, the right hand side,
> or the cost. Some of the more usual methods of reducing
> the effects of uncertainty are (1) replacing the random
> elements by their expected values, (2) replacing the
> random elements by pessimistic estimates of their
> values, and (3) recasting the problem into a two-stage
> problem where, in the second stage, one can compensate
> for "inaccuracies" in the first stage activities. These
> methods are called the expected value solution, "fat"
> solution, and "slack" solution, respectively.

Other methods that will be presented here are: Contini's approach,
chance-constraint approach, Evers' approach, and Charnes-Stedry's
approach.

The "Expected Value" Solution

As stated before, the goal programming problem might be
expressed as

Min: $D = \Sigma \alpha_i^+ d_i^+ + \alpha_i^- d_i^-$ (4.41)

Subject to: $Ax - 1d^+ + 1d^- = b$ (4.42)

$0 \leq x \leq 1$ (4.43)

The stochastic elements may be associated with the investment-opportunity or the source-of-funds matrixes, the goal vector (b), or the vector of weights (α). To replace the parametric values by their expected values, a detailed analysis of the probability functions—discrete or continuous—must be performed. For example, the investment-opportunity matrix (A) might be totally stochastic in nature, or only partly stochastic. This case of uncertainty may represent a situation in which locational impacts of different investment projects are stochastically determined. If project x_1 is located in region R_1, the value, for example, of the employment generation may be represented by a_{ij}; but if project x_1 is located in region R_2, it may generate only b_{ij} units of employment. Probabilities are defined to the location in R_1 or R_2. In particular, assume that there is a probability p that project x_1 be located in R_1 and $1 - p$ if located in R_2 (a more complex probability function in a multiregion locational game may be defined).

The expected value of employment generation by project x_1 is equal to $c_{ij} = p^* a_{ij} + (1 - p)^* b_{ij}$. The investment-opportunity matrix, then, can also be separated in submatrixes where one part presents those nonstochastic elements, and the other the stochastic ones (Evers 1967).

For example, the problem can be stated as:

Min: $D = \Sigma \alpha_i^+ d_i^+ + \alpha_i^- d_i^-$ (4.44)

Subject to: $A_1 x - 1d^+ + 1d^- = b_1$ (4.45)

$A_2 x - 1d^+ + 1d^- = b_2$ (4.46)

$0 \leq x \leq 1$ or $\Sigma x_j = 1$ (4.47)

where b_2 represents a stochastic vector of goals and A_2 represents the expected value of the coefficients. When the expected-value solution is applied to all of matrix A, it does not mean that the same probability function is used for different types of impacts. The reason for emphasizing this point is the fact that the random elements associated with employment, for example, may be related to a set of stochastic variables that are not associated to the same stochastic variables of other attributes.

The "Fat" Solution

In practice, this is one of the most common approaches for dealing with uncertainty. The method consists of assuming pessimistic values for the parameters in the A, b, or α vectors. Once these values are determined, the problem becomes nonstochastic and the procedure is the same as in the case without uncertainty.

One of the main problems in choosing the pessimistic values of the x's relates to their feasibility and permanency. We know that, given (A, b), all the x's that will satisfy the constraints will form a convex polyhedron. All these pessimistic values chosen must fulfill this condition.

"If only b is random, the intersection is easily described. Let b* be the vector whose ith element is the supremum of the ith coordinates of the possible vectors b. Then, the sets of x's satisfying $Ax \le b^*$, $x \ge 0$, [in our case, $Ax - 1d^+ + 1d^- = b^*$, $x \ge 0$] are a subset of the set of permanently feasible x's" (Madansky 1962, p. 467). In practice these procedures are carried out through the use of sensitivity analysis in a trial-error form.

The "Slack" Solution

This method is very similar to the way in which goal programming solved the basic problem. Lee (1972, p. 178) states that "in fact, goal programming may even be a special case of the slack method under conditions of fairly certain expected values in the A-matrix and b-vector. But with the slack method, A and b are subject to random variations. The only apparent difference between this approach and goal programming is the random variations of A and b and the fact that the choice of variables appear in the objective function."

Consider the polyhedra $Ax \ge b$, x 0, with A and b being random. A problem may be stated as

Min c'x or E c'x   (4.48)

Subject to $Ax \ge b$ (4.49)

$\qquad x \ge 0$

For any infeasible solution x, a penalty cost is associated to it of f'y; where $y \ge 0$ and f' is the penalty cost per unit of infeasibility y. This penalty cost is then incorporated into the objective function of the programming problem.

Madansky (1962) states the problem in the following way:

$$E \min_{y}: \quad (c'x - f'y) \tag{4.50}$$

Subject to: $AX + By = b$ (4.51)

$$x \geq 0, y \geq 0 \tag{4.52}$$

where A and B are random matrixes, and B is known, and x and y
are n_1 and n_2 dimensional vectors. It is possible immediately to
see the relationship between the y's and the d_i^+'s in the GP model.
They have the same orthogonality properties, where c' is a vector
exactly equal to 0. The slack solution is taken from the role of the
y's which, in a sense, represent slack variables which will be
"compensators" for inaccuracies in the decision (f'y represents a
penalty cost).

The similarity of this method with GP becomes clear when
analyzing the behavioral variability of the vector y. This vector
may take positive and negative values (y^+ and y^-) and is mathematically
defined by

$$y \begin{cases} y^+ = b - Ax \\ y^- = 0 \end{cases} \text{if } b \geq Ax \quad \text{or } y \begin{cases} y^+ = 0 \\ y^- = Ax - b \end{cases} \text{if } b < Ax \tag{4.53}$$

Contini's Approach

Contini (1968) states that the first step in dealing with uncertainty
is to relax the assumption of a fixed relation between the target variable y and all the instruments associated with it (in the present problem this y variable corresponds to b, the goal vector). In other words,
he states that

$$Y = Ax + u \tag{4.54}$$

where u is a random vector normally distributed with mean 0 and
variance-covariance Σ, A is a matrix of fixed coefficients, and Σ
is assumed to be a known nonsingular variance-covariance matrix.
Then, $y \sim N(Ax, \Sigma)$. With this normality assumption, the GP problem is to minimize a quadratic form of the type:

$$\text{Min: } \Delta = (y^* - Ax)'\Sigma^{-1} (y^* - Ax) \tag{4.55}$$

subject to the other technical constraints of the GP problem.

After several transformations of the expression, it comes to be of the following type:

$$\Delta = y^{*'}\Sigma^{-1}y^* + x'A'\Sigma^{-1}Ax - 2y^*\Sigma^{-1}Ax \qquad (4.56)$$

Let $k = y^{*'}\Sigma^{-1}y^*$, which implies that

$$\Delta = k + x'Rx + 2p'x \qquad (4.57)$$

$$R = A'\Sigma^{-1}A \qquad (4.58)$$

$$P = -A'\Sigma^{-1}y^* \qquad (4.59)$$

and $\Delta^* = y^{*'}\Sigma^{-1}(y^* - Ax^*)$, expression of the optimal value of Δ^* as a function of the discrepancy between the target vector (goals) and the vector of means Ax (project attributes). The first order conditions for minimizing are

$$\frac{d\Delta}{dx} = 2Rx + 2p = 0 \qquad R_1x = -p \qquad (4.60)$$

where, if R is nonsingular,

$$x^* = -R^{-1}p \text{ or } x^* = (A'\Sigma'A)^{-1}A'\Sigma^{-1}y^* \qquad (4.61)$$

This expression has a very close resemblance to the value of the slope coefficient given by the generalized least square in multiple regression analysis.

This whole condition of optimality, and so the applicability of this method, depends upon the singularity of R, which in turn depends on the number of equations and instruments involved in the basic statement of the GP problem.

Chance-Constraint Approach

Sengupta and Gruver (1969, p. 221) state that

a linear programming (LP) problem is said to have chance-constraints, if its constraints have a finite probability of being violated. The chance-constrainted programming (CCP) approach develops a method of providing appropriate safety margins under chance-constraints, by incorporating the distributional characteristics of the random variables of the problem, e.g., the resource vector and the input-output coefficients. In this method a tolerance level (in terms of a probability measure), one for which probabilistic constraint is preassigned by the decision makers and this set of tolerance measures is supposed to indicate the limit up to which constraint violations are permitted.

To offer a solution to this problem, Charnes and Cooper (1959) state that the problem may be divided into two major steps: the determination of the coefficients of the stochastic functions, and the parameters which will drive to the optimal decision rules.

In the simplest case—randomness associated with the vectors of goals b_i—the problem of chance constraint is stated as

$$\text{Max } z = c'x \tag{4.62}$$

$$\text{Subject to } a_i x \leq b_i \tag{4.63}$$
$$\qquad\qquad i = 1, 2, \ldots, m$$
$$\qquad x \geq 0$$

where a_i is the ith column of the matrix A, where b_i is assumed to be random and probabilistically mutually exclusive and independent. The cumulative distribution function is:

$$F(a_i x) = \text{Prob}(b_i \leq a_i x) = 1 - u_i;\ 0 < u_i < 1 \tag{4.64}$$

The reliability measure R_1 is defined in terms of the probability that the ith goal will be violated:

$$R_i = u_i = \text{Prob}\ (b_i \geq a_i x) = 1 - F(a_i x) \tag{4.65}$$

Given a set of known nonnegative constant weights, w_1 and w_2, the transformed programming problem which incorporates the system reliability is presented by

$$\text{Max } U = w_1 c'x + w_2\ \log u_i \tag{4.66}$$

$$R_i(a_i x) - u_i = 0 \tag{4.67}$$

$$0 \leq u_i \leq 1$$
$$\qquad x \geq 0 \qquad i = 1, 2, \ldots, n$$

where $R_i(a_i x) = \text{Prob}(b_i \geq a_i x)$. Assumptions regarding the distribution of b_i will finally determine the expression of the problem.

The same type of methodology may be applied to investment decision making in which a specific probability is chance-constrained to a particular equation or structural constraint of the problem.

Evers' Approach

Evers (1967) criticized the use of the "fat" solution because of the nature of some decisions where the range of variability is very small to which "plenty of fat" might permit a drive toward a sub-optimal solution. He was mainly concerned with the analytics of stochastic elements associated with the a_{ij} coefficients in the A matrix (here, the investment-opportunity matrix).

The general problem may be stated as

$$\text{Min:} \quad C^T x \tag{4.68}$$

$$\text{Subject to:} \quad Ax \geq B \tag{4.69}$$

$$x \geq 0 \tag{4.70}$$

Evers then separated the stochastic elements of the A matrix by a partition into two sets of constraints. The transformation of the problem is stated as follows:

$$\text{Min}_x: \quad C^T x \tag{4.71}$$

$$\text{Subject to:} \quad A_1 x \geq B_1 \tag{4.72}$$

$$A_2 x \geq B_2 \tag{4.73}$$

$$x \geq 0 \tag{4.74}$$

The chance-constraint formulation is accomplished by defining a set T^* such that the following probability function is met:

$$T^* = [x: \Pr(A_1 x \geq B_1) \geq \gamma; \ 0 \leq \gamma \leq 1, \ x \geq 0] \tag{4.75}$$

This chance-constraint elaboration is then transformed to reflect stochastic behaviors in the objective function. In this new elaboration of the objective function, Evers introduces a new notation into the vector X. Let X_1 belong to T^*; X_2 be a deficiency variable; and X_3 a slack variable. The characteristics of these vectors are

$$X_2^{(s)} = \begin{cases} B_1^{(s)} - A_1^{(s)} x_1 & \text{if } A_1^{(s)} x_1 < B_1^{(s)} \ s\epsilon s \\ 0 \text{ otherwise} & \text{(s denotes the rank of} \\ & \text{the partition)} \end{cases} \quad (4.76)$$

Then,

$$A_1 x_1 + x_2 \geq B_1 \tag{4.77}$$

$$A_2 x_1 - x_3 = B_2 \tag{4.78}$$

$$x_1, \, x_2, \, x_3 \geq 0 \tag{4.79}$$

In the chance-constraint approach, different values of T^* were found, depending upon a specified value of $\gamma = \gamma_0$. In this case, the γ values are part of the optimization problem. This optimization process is carried out by defining a different type of cost function which will take into consideration not only $C^T x$, but also the expression associated with the expected value of shortage $K^T G(X)$, and the costs associated with M. These effects are incorporated into the objective function by stating the problem as

$$\underset{x}{\text{Min}}: \qquad [C^T s + K^T G(x) + M(1 - \gamma(x))] \tag{4.80}$$

Subject to: $A_2 x \geq B_2 \tag{4.81}$

$$x \geq 0 \tag{4.82}$$

where $1 - \gamma$ represents the $\Pr(X_2^{(s)}) > 0$.

Charnes–Stedry Approach

The introduction of uncertainty into the problem allows the decision maker to minimize the expected value of the R function, where, for simplicity, the probability of obtaining a d_j^+ is P, and the probability of getting a d_j^- is $(1 - P)$. For a generalization of this probability function, assume a probability P_i for the different d_j^+, and $(1 - P_i)$ for the respective d_j^-. Moreover, any other probability function may be attached to the expected behavior of the d_j^+ and d_j^-, r_j and p_j being rewards and penalties.

The expected value of R is

$$E(d_j^+) + (1) \, P(x_j \geq g_j) + (0) \, [1 - P\{x_j \geq g_j\}] \tag{4.83}$$

$$E(\bar{d}_j) + (0)\ P(x_j \geq g_j) + (1)\ [1 - P\{x_j \geq g_j\}]\ \qquad (4.84)$$

Then

$$E(R) + \sum_{j=1}^{n}\ (r_j + p_j)b_j(1 - e^{-\alpha j\rho j}) - \Sigma P_j \qquad (4.85)$$

where g_j is the set of goals, x_j represents the set of decision variables (the performance of the jth investment activity), ρ_j is the effort allocated in area j, and α_j is a parameter of this function. Further details of the probability of goal attainment functions can be found in Charnes and Stedry (1964).

TIME AS AN ENDOGENOUS VARIABLE

Since time is incorporated in the decision model, there are two choices in utilizing the results: (1) employ the present value of all streams of income and cost, which requires the specification of a discount rate; or (2) achieve each of the goal levels at least to the level of the specified target in each period, here the issue of a discount rate is avoided. The goal may be to maximize the net present value of future income, or it may be to achieve an income level at least as large as the preestablished goal in each period. In using the former case, there is an explicit need to specify the appropriate discount rate to be used, in spite of the fact that impacts associated with changes in the discount rate upon the optimal solution may be known by means of a sensitivity analysis. In the latter case, there is no need to specify the discount rate; rather, in comparing year-by-year values, a dual evaluator is used (Ijiri 1965).

Ijiri defines a dual evaluator as an index of the changes in the objective function due to simultaneous changes in one constraint when relaxed by one unit. That is, the dual evaluator incorporates a mutatis mutandis concept of opportunity costs rather than a ceteris paribus concept. The ceteris paribus concept considers variations in one of the variables assuming all other variables constant, whereas the mutatis mutandis concept of opportunity costs assumes that all variables are optimally adjusted. "This is, in fact, the intended meaning of the term 'mutatis mutandis' which has been accorded to this way of reckoning opportunity costs, in contrast to other approaches which assume that only a few variables are adjusted while all others are held constant" (Ijiri 1965, p. 124).

The inclusion of the time variable transforms the GP problem into

$$\text{Min:} \quad D = \sum_{i=1}^{m} \sum_{t=1}^{s} p_{ti}^{+} d_{it}^{+} + p_{ti}^{-} d_{it}^{-} \qquad (4.86)$$

$$\text{Subject to:} \quad A_t x - 1d_t^{+} - 1d_t^{-} = b_t \qquad (4.87)$$

$$x, d_t^{+}, d_t^{-} \geq 0 \qquad (4.88)$$

THE UTILITY APPROACH TO
PROJECT FORMULATION

The first element that must be analyzed to assess preferences is the real bundle of project alternatives. These can be actual (already in operation) or potential investment activities; this is to say that the definition of alternatives does not necessarily constrain the decision maker to activities that have already been implemented.

Each alternative must be evaluated in terms of what is called "measures of effectiveness"—here referred to as "attributes." They are characteristics attached to each of the objectives through which effectiveness can be determined by the use of more than one attribute. In cases like transportation projects, the alternatives to the decision maker may be represented by three types of projects: air, railroad, and truck; while the attributes may be represented by noise levels, safety, comfort, and the like. Moreover, comfort, for example, may be represented by more than one characteristic: seat volume, time, or any other relevant element incorporated in the analysis.

All of the attributes are incorporated into a well-defined welfare function to be maximized, given the technical specifications of the alternative bundles. The final vector of activities chosen will be that one which maximizes the welfare function. Details about the determination of this welfare function will be given later.

At this stage of the analysis two more elements are important for consideration: incidence, and trade-offs between different measures of effectiveness. Most of the attributes which will define a particular measure of effectiveness can be classified by their incidence to three types of groups: general government, user, and nonuser. The grouping of attributes by their incidence is a very important factor for policy decisions (Keeney 1973). The analysis of trade-offs between different measures of effectiveness will answer the question: How much of a particular measure of effectiveness does the economy have to sacrifice in order to improve its position by one unit in another measure of effectiveness? This trade-off analysis is generally studied in the determination of indifference curves.

Indifference Curves

In project selection the decision maker has to make two types of indifference analyses: the role of real valued attributes, and financial alternatives (different sources of funds) (MacCrimmon 1969). In utility analysis these are called "iso-preferences" and "iso-budget" analyses, respectively.

The first steps in the indifference analysis are represented by the definition of "the goal structure" since it may differ from one unit to the other, the explanation of the goal hierarchy, and the possible interdependence of goals (MacCrimmon 1969). In defining attribute values, MacCrimmon defines two main concepts: "feasibility" and "acceptability." The application of a feasible and acceptable level of a particular attribute will constrain the set of values to a relevant set to which preference functions can be defined.

Given the available budget and other technological constraints, it is possible to define, over each attribute, the infeasible and unacceptable regions. For example, it is stated that in bus transportation ambient noise cannot be reduced to less than 40 decibels, and that 80 decibels represents an unacceptable level. The same type of analysis may be done for each of the attributes. Finally, they can be represented graphically in what is called a "circular feasibility/acceptability chart" (MacCrimmon 1969).

This chart will allow the decision maker to relate different attributes and to find the real trade-offs, given the set of preference functions. For example, in Figure 4.5 a hypothetical example of ambient noise and travel time trade-offs is traced for a particular type of transportation system. The lower the ambient noise and the lower the time spent in traveling, the better off a consumer of transportation services is. This description will determine the direction of preferences.

The direction of preferences described by Figure 4.5 is only one of the possible representations of these trade-offs. In Figure 4.6 a range of different potential trade-offs is presented. The usual limitation of the graphical analysis of trade-offs is the impossibility of describing them when more dimensions are introduced.

Following the previously discussed analysis, the decision maker must determine the multiattributed utility function that will serve as the basic notion of society's welfare. The assessment of this function will depend upon the specific assumptions of the decision maker.

This general welfare function can be stated as

$$W(x) = U[u_1(x_1), u_2(x_2), \ldots, u_n(x_n)] \qquad (4.89)$$

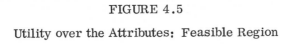

FIGURE 4.5

Utility over the Attributes: Feasible Region

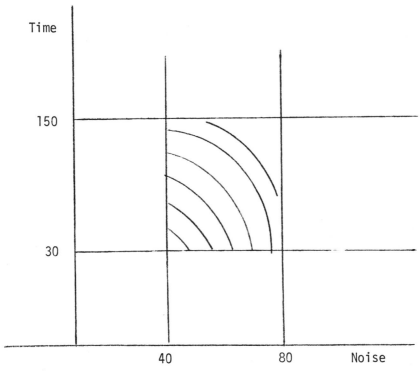

Source: Compiled by the authors.

In order to make it operational, assumptions with respect to utility, preferences, and probability (when under uncertainty) between the attributes must be defined. If probability, utility, and preference independence are assumed, two types of welfare functions may be used: additive, and multiplicative (Keeney 1971 and 1973). They are of the following form:

$$W(x) = u_1(x_1) + u_2(x_2) + \ldots + u_n(x_n) \qquad (4.90)$$

$$W(x) = u_1(x_1) \times u_2(x_2) \times \ldots \times u_n(x_n) \qquad (4.91)$$

The holding of these particular assumptions is an empirical question that requires verification. In general, these types of welfare functions are used for simplicity in the calculation.

FIGURE 4.6

Utility over the Attributes:
Direction of Preferences

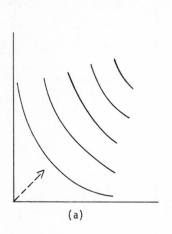

(a)

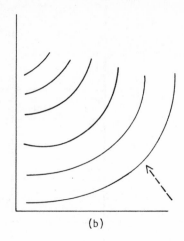

(b)

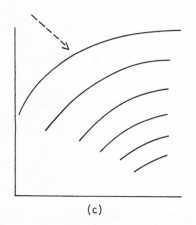

(c)

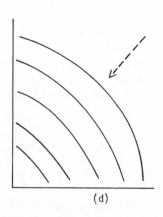

(d)

Source: Compiled by the authors.

The next step in the analysis is the verification of the "independ-ence" assumptions. Once this step is accomplished, it is necessary to define each of the $u(x_i)$ that are the basic arguments of those utility functions. The method suggested by Keeney (1973) was developed by Schlaifer (1969), and consists of assessing infeasible and unacceptable levels, in an action-probability space, for each of the variables under analysis. The final step relates to the evaluation of all possible welfare levels, given the multiple alternatives of the problem, and the selection of that alternative which maximizes the total welfare of the economy.

The Lexicographic Approach

This is a special case of the direct assessed preference approach. Two models will be presented in this section: the "Additive Model" and the "Additive Difference Model" (Tversky 1969). A choice be-tween these two alternatives (projects x_1 and x_2) implies finding a decision rule which will determine when x_1 is preferred to x_2, or vice versa. Two methods can be used to choose between the alterna-tives. One assumes independence between the alternatives, and the other compares the intrinsic characteristics of the two alternatives, analyzing the components' differences among the x's.

The first method evaluates x_1 and x_2 separately and defines a utility function U over the alternatives. In the final analysis, x_1 will be preferred to x_2 if and only if $U(x_1) > U(x_2)$.

If there exists a real value function U_i, $i = 1, 2, \ldots, n$ such that x_1 is preferred to x_2 if and only if $U(x_1) = \sum_j U(a_{ij})$ is greater than $U(x_2) = \sum_j U(a_{2j})$, then activity one is chosen over activity two.

This is the criterion behind the additive model.

In the second model, a difference function must be defined. For example, activity one will be preferred to activity two if and only if the following relation is fulfilled:

$$\sum_{i=1}^{n} q_i [u_i(z_i^1) - U_i(z_i^2)] > 0 \qquad (4.92)$$

where

$$q_i(-e) = -q_i(e) \, \forall_i \qquad (4.93)$$

$$e = U_i(z_i^1), \; z_i \text{ (attribute i)} \qquad (4.94)$$

The difference functions may assume any shape.

The advantage of the additive model over the additive difference model resides in the fact that the strictly additive model will always satisfy the transitivity requirements imposed by the basic axioms of utility theory. The negative additive model will satisfy the transitivity axiom when the number of activities is greater than or equal to three, if and only if all difference functions are linear (Tversky 1969).

Limitations

There are some limitations to the utility approach to project formulation that are relevant to mention at this point. First, the real incorporation of attributes into the utility functions for the assessment of preferences is not always feasible. Meaningful information, within marginal analysis, is rarely collected by planning agencies. The successful assessment of preferences essentially depends upon the specification of two basic elements: (1) the clear determination of the true direction of preferences and, then, the behavioral variability of the attributes as functions of the direction of preferences (that is, the higher the noise level the less preferable a particular transportation system, and preferences will decline faster at higher levels of noise); and (2) the time span in which the attribute intensities are set (decibels per second during X hours). Attribute performance and time span are difficult to combine in complex systems of formulation.

Second, given the difficulty in obtaining meaningful data for use in the assessment of preferences, the utility approach in the context of multiple attributed alternatives weakens–especially multiattributed alternatives in the context of multivariety and multipurpose projects. This phenomenon becomes more important when the process of investment formulation considers projects of a very different nature (agricultural, industrial, transportation). It seems that this approach works more effectively under situations in which the decision maker is choosing among projects of the same nature in the framework of mutually exclusiveness. Otherwise, trade-offs in the process of preference assessments become unmanageable. This becomes particularly important when information on preferences, among states of a given attribute and preferences across attributes, is required.

The first two limitations introduce serious methodological shortcomings at the operational level of model building. In order to cope with the limitations–the availability and quality of data, and the excessive attributes varieties–those models are implemented with assumptions that allow the economist/planner to justify the use of additive or multiplicative social welfare functions. To have an additive or multiplicative utility function there must be assumed utility, preference, and probability (when dealing with uncertainty) independence. Otherwise, it becomes impossible to define the appropriate form of the utility function. The validity of these assumptions is, of course, empirical in nature and they become more inappropriate the larger and the more interdependent the projects (or set of projects) under consideration.

Finally, at the planning level, this type of model is very difficult to integrate with other decision-making models which are aggregate and statistical in nature. In planning agencies, the typical models are of the type of national income accounts, input-output, and sources and uses of funds.

SUMMARY

This chapter has presented the mathematical formulation of the proposed decision-making model. Goal programming is an adequate model for policy makers because of how the objective function is specified, and because it can incorporate, as an integral part of the method, national income models via the goal vector and the budget constraint.

In the first part GP was compared with LP, the latter being a very commonly used technique. The references to LP have focused upon the basic programming model because GP may represent (although not always) a linear transformation of LP programs. The ability of GP to deal with these procedures is not constrained to linear forms; quadratic objective functions can be used and computers can easily handle this type of program. Also, parametric, integer, and dynamic programming are now available. The determination of using any of these models depends upon the decision-making environment and the general efficiency gained by using these transformations.

A brief presentation was made of GP and uncertainty. Although the "expected value" solution was employed, other methods are possible and may be incorporated. This chapter did not cover duality questions (that is, dual variables) because the presentation in Chapter 3 is easily generalized to the presentation of GP within a multiobjective framework.

REFERENCES

Charnes, A. and A. Stedry. 1964. "Investigations in the Theory of Multiple Budgeted Goals." In Management Controls: New Directions in Basic Research, ed. C. P. Bonini, R. K. Jaekicke, and H. M. Wagner. New York: McGraw-Hill.

Charnes, A., and W. W. Cooper. 1959. "Chance-Constrained Programming." Management Science 6, no. 2 (October): 73-79.

Contini, Bruno. 1968. "A Stochastic Approach to Goal Programming." Operation Research 16, no. 3 (May-June): 576-86.

Dawes, Robyn Mason. 1964. "Social Selection Based on Multidimensional Criteria." Journal of Abnormal Social Psychology 68, no. 1: 104-09.

Evers, William H. 1967. "A New Model for Stochastic Linear Programming." Management Science 13, no. 9 (May): 680-93.

Haimes, Y. Y., and Warren A. Hall. 1974. "Multiobjectives in Water Resource Systems Analysis: The Surrogate-Worth Trade Off Methods." Water Resources Research 10, no. 4 (August): 615-34.

Haimes, Y. Y., W. A. Hall, and H. T. Freedman. 1975. Multiobjective Optimization in Water Resources Systems. New York: Elsevier.

Hawkins, Clark A., and Richard A. Adams. 1974. "A Goal Programming Model for Capital Budgeting." Financial Management, Spring, pp. 52-57.

Ijiri, Y. 1965. Management Goals and Accounting for Control. Amsterdam: North Holland Publishing Co.

IDB/UNDP (Inter-American Development Bank/UN Development Program). 1975. "Mid-project Evaluation Workshop." June, Washington, D.C.

ILO. 1972. "Creacion de Empleo y Absorcion de Desempled En Chile: La Experiencia de 1971." United Nations, International Labor Office, Geneva.

Kenney, Ralph L. 1971. "Utility Independence and Preferences for Multiattributed Consequences." Operations Research 19: 875-93.

_____. 1973. "Concepts of Independence in Multiattribute Utility Theory." In Multiple Criteria Decision Making, ed. J. L. Cochrane and M. Zeleny. Columbia: University of South Carolina Press.

Lee, Sang M. 1971. "Decision Analysis Through Goal Programming."
Decision Sciences 2 (April): 172-80.

_____. 1972. Goal Programming for Decision Analysis. Philadelphia:
Auerbach Publishers.

MacCrimmon, Kenneth R. 1969. Improving the System Design and
Evaluation Process by the Use of Trade-off Information: An
Application to Northeast Corridor Transportation Planning,
RM-5877. Santa Monica, Calif.: Rand Corporation, April.

Madansky, A. 1962. "Methods of Solution of Linear Programs
Under Uncertainty." Operations Research 10, no. 4 (July-
August): 463-71.

Major, David. 1969. "Benefit-Cost Ratios for Projects in Multiple
Objective Investment Programs." Water Resources Research 5,
no. 6, pp. 1174-78.

Nikaido, H. 1972. Introduction to Sets and Mappings in Modern
Economics. Amsterdam: North Holland Publishing Co.

Papandreou, A., and U. Zohar. 1974. The Impact Approach to
Project Selection: Volume II. New York: Praeger.

Schlaifer, R. O. 1969. Analysis of Decisions Under Uncertainty.
New York: McGraw-Hill.

Sengupta, J. K., and G. Gruver. 1969. "A Linear Reliability
Analysis in Programming with Chance Constraints." Swedish
Journal of Economics 71, no. 2: 221-46.

Tversky, A. 1969. "Intransitivity of Preferences." Psychological
Review 76: 31-48.

CHAPTER

5

BASIS FOR A
DATA SYSTEM

Our method focuses on a level of aggregation which is based on projects' contributions to economic development. These investment characteristics involve considerations such as income, employment, foreign exchange, and the like. The level of aggregation will determine the significance of the quantitative and qualitative aspects of the required information, a factor usually forgotten when comparing investment criteria that respond to different levels of aggregation.

These attributes may be set up in a one-to-one relation with each of the predetermined objectives. In particular, if growth of national income represents an objective, the respective column in the investment-opportunity matrix would represent levels of income generated by each of the investment alternatives. For simplicity, a one-to-one relation between social objectives and the project's attributes has been assumed.

When more than one component might be representing or contributing to a unique objective, principal component analysis will allow the planner to come to a "unique" index, in a one-to-one fashion, with the objective under consideration. Principal component analysis is a statistical technique which allows decision makers to determine a set of weights, for a given number of variables, based on the implicit correlation of those variables. Weights are chosen so that the index will explain as much as possible of the variance of the variables.

Assume that the planner is interested in determining an index of regional income, and that there are five "explanatory" variables and 15 projects. Thus, there are 5×15 observation (matrix X), and the values of the index for each of the projects will form a 15×1 matrix (C). The set of weights (W) to apply to the regional income index satisfy

$$C' = W'X \qquad\qquad\qquad (5.1)$$

Subject to: $W'W = 1$ (standardization of the weights)

If E represents the matrix of variances and covariances of the original variables, the method consists of maximizing the variance matrix of the C observations, $V(C)$, which in a Lagrangian form is

$$\text{Max } L = W'EW - \lambda(W'W - 1) \qquad\qquad (5.2)$$

This solution implies $|E - \lambda I| = 0$, where λ is the characteristic root (eigenvalue) of W. The largest value of λ is used to solve for the set of weights (W).*
Once the attributes that will characterize each of the investment alternatives are identified, a second step should follow: determination of the direction of preferences over those attributes. Increasing or decreasing direction of preferences may be defined over the same attribute, depending upon the economic state under consideration. In particular, a country's merits may be set over increasing levels of absorption of a certain type of labor or level of income, while the opposite merits, of the same attribute, may be defined in other countries. It is up to the policy maker to decide. In order to test the performance of the decision-making model, it has been assumed that the direction of preferences are known by the economist/planner.

Two formats will be presented here: The investment-opportunity matrix (IOM) and the source-of-funds matrix (SOFM). The IOM lists in its rows the proposed projects, and in its columns the policy maker's objectives. The SOFM also considers sources of foreign funds in its rows, and their statistical attributes (characteristics) in its columns.

The following section of the chapter will focus on the IOM and alternative definitions of its elements such as income, employment, and foreign exchange; then the last section will do the same conceptual analysis for the statistical attributes of borrowed funds such as interest rate, grace period, maturity, and the like.

INVESTMENT-OPPORTUNITY MATRIX

The format of the investment-opportunity matrix consists of rows which list all existing and potential projects that are under consideration. The columns represent a list of different attributes

---

*For more references to this topic, see Morrison (1967).

that characterize the impacts of each of the investment opportunities, over time, to the objectives of society. Three main advantages of this format warrant mention. First, the possibility of incorporating a multidimensional set of attributes, which relates to society's objectives, will allow a very clear and effective way of introducing a multiple objective formulation model. Second, the format will serve as a meaningful informational system for government planners and decision makers in the light of a multiobjective framework. Finally, because it represents an informational system, the format will play a crucial role in the implementation and postevaluation of the investment plan in the economy.

To put these figures into operation not all possible attributes are included in the analysis. The basic reason is that the model represents a methodological proposition, and a more simplified format will allow a clearer exposition of the analysis. Second, tentative forms of representing particular attributes are considered. They do not represent definite ways of conceptualizing the indicators that are particularly useful for planning decisions. This implies that extensive definitions are not given and accurate and detailed formulas to insure these attributes are not found in this chapter. The main purpose of this chapter is to explain how to construct this matrix to allow operation of the multiobjective decision model.

Taking these aspects into consideration, this chapter will focus on three main indicators, to which some forms of measurement are suggested: income, employment, and foreign exchange.

Attribute One: Income

Sometimes, implicitly or explicitly, income has been used as a primary indicator of economic welfare. Comparisons of different levels of income in a particular country or comparison of different countries' income levels are examples. This is not to say that agreement has been reached in terms of the "best" connotations or denotations of the word income. To obtain a flavor for what different economists mean by income, some definitions of the term will be presented.

Various Definitions

Irving Fisher says that "income is a series of events" (1969, p. 33). He also differentiates some psychic, real, and monetary concepts of income. He states that "events—the psychic experiences of the individual mind . . . constitute ultimate income for that individual" (1969, p. 33). The concept of income as a psychological

entity induces economists to approximate and to measure this concept
indirectly. Fisher stated that this indirect approximation is called
"real" income (that is, shelter, clothes, food). In recognition of
difficulties in measuring psychological enjoyment, he proposes the
concept of cost of living as a measure of real income: "The total
cost of living, in the sense of money payments, is a negative item,
being outgo rather than income; but is our best practical measure
of the positive items of real income for which those payments are
made" (1969, p. 35). Furthermore, Fisher distinguishes between
the cost of a commodity and the cost of its use, saying that "we
should always calculate the value of 'service,' and never the value
of the objects rendering those services" (1969, p. 36).

Lindahl (1969) distinguished four different concepts of income:
(1) income as consumption: "services obtained from capital goods
during a certain period" (p. 54); (2) income as interest: "the continuous appreciation of capital goods owing to the time factor, that
is to say, the current interest on capital value which the goods
represent" (p. 55); (3) income as earnings: "the sum of the actual
consumption and the increase of capital value which has taken place
during a certain period" (p. 58); and (4) income as produce, which
is defined "analogously to the concept of production" (p. 59).

Hicks (1969, pp. 76-77) presented three definitions of income,
which serve as a base for welfare judgments:

> Income No. 1 is the maximum amount which can be
> spent during a period if there is to be an expectation
> of maintaining intact the capital value of prospective
> receipts in money terms. Income No. 2 as the maxi-
> mum amount the individual can spend this week and
> still expect to be able to spend the same amount in
> each ensuing week. Income No. 3 as the maximum
> amount of money which an individual can spend this
> week, and still expect to be able to spend the same
> amount 'in real terms' in each ensuing week.

It is possible to see that these definitions basically are presenting concepts of income related to the realization of some economic
activity: services derived from goods and commodities, through
direct or indirect consumption; and income from earnings by salaries,
wages, interest, or any other source of "income."

In considering the incorporation of "income" as an important
attribute of each of the projects under analysis, the main concern
is twofold: First, to have a basic measure of social welfare; and
second, to introduce into the model a programming approach to
income that will enable planners to incorporate other variables into

the formulation model. These two concepts induce one to think in
terms of the familiar concept of social or national income. This is
to say that projects will be distinguished by how much income they
generate in each of the years considered by the formulation plan.
    Simons (1969, pp. 65-66) stated that

> social income denotes, broadly, a measure of the net
> results of economic activity in a community during a
> specified period of time. . . . the social income might
> be conceived in terms either of the value of goods and
> services produced or of the value of the productive
> services utilized during the period (after deduction
> for depreciation and depletion). . . . In short, social
> income is merely a welfare conception. To say that
> it has increased is to say that things which must be
> economized are more abundant (or, perhaps, are
> utilized with greater "efficiency"). . . . Increase in
> the social income suggests progress toward "the good
> life," toward a world better in its economic aspects,
> whatever that may be; and it is precisely as definite
> and measurable as is such progress.

These definitions do not exclude measurement of income, depending upon project location in the income flow, the problem under
consideration, and the availability of data. To use the increase in
income per capita, national income, disposable income, and other
"measures of welfare" are not excluded.

Regional Income

The income impact of a project in a region gives a different
dimension to the attribute. The concept of income has been explained
already; what is necessary now is to try to conceptualize "region."
To present the regional income impact of projects calls for the
regionalization of the country. The conceptualization of the "region"
in development planning has not been satisfactory. One of the main
limitations is associated with the fact that requirements for the
development of regions are greater than the real availability of
existent resources of the region.
    An acceptable definition of region will serve as the following
base: (1) to direct investments and develop certain natural resources,
(2) to establish "growth" poles, (3) to coordinate development of
infrastructural facilities (highways, dams), and (4) to balance economic growth between urban and rural areas (Waterston 1974).

The basic question is how to define, identify, and divide different parts of an economy in order to make a meaningful plan for different economic fluctuations, growth, and development. A region generally refers to a portion of a country that has been well-defined in terms of some specified criteria, one of which is the division of a country by the endowment of natural resources. This division has the advantage that programming may be made of the allocation and use of these resources. Also, it centers the investment process in a direction of full service and utilization of certain resources. The main disadvantage relates to the multiplicity of resources in a particular geographical area and the highly diversified demand of different resources by one investment project.

Related to this definition of a region, the division of a country by capital and human resources may also be taken into consideration. The main advantage of this is that capital represents one of the most scarce resources with labor one of the most abundant. This apparent dichotomy makes this capital-labor criterion an important one in development planning. The abundance of labor in certain parts of these countries calls attention to regionalization, taking into consideration the actual configuration of "pockets of poverty." As far as employment is concerned, it will be analyzed in the next section. Here, the basic proposition relates to dividing the country in regions of different per capita income.

One of the most widely used criteria for regionalizing a country is climate. In countries such as Brazil, Argentina, and Chile, where almost all types of climate exist, the regionalization of the country under this criterion would have a direct relation to potential development of certain types of output. Irrigation and transportation, for example, have a different character, depending upon their location (that is, technical standards and feasibility).

To regionalize a country by basic economic sectors is very common. The "industrial" region, or the "agricultural" region, is a frequent classification in regional analysis. This type of concept relates directly to the degree of specialization—basically, types of output—of a geographical area. The historical advantage of this criterion, in the early stages of a developing country's economic development, is in doubt when technology and development of "mixed" sectors (for example, agroindustry) are taking place.

Finally, there is the criterion for regionalization based upon political jurisdiction. Under this criterion, the basic unit most generally is represented by "the village," where the intermediate unit is represented by the "municipality," and the largest unit is represented by the "province." This division is particularly important in terms of political participation and government budget alloca-

tion. This criterion seems very important for improving the rural
development of certain government services which are crucially
important during the implementation stages of the projects.

In order to have orderly growth and development of certain
areas, to establish the adequate "growth poles" to counterbalance
economic concentration, and to program and implement the allocation
and use of potential resources, regionalization calls for a combination of the resource endowment and the jurisdictional criteria;
although explicit recognition of the pockets-of-poverty criterion is
very important in the low-income economies.

It remains to say that the problem and the country under consideration will give basic elements to discriminate between the
criteria. Finally, sensitivity analysis may be made to assumptions
of different criteria, which will allow planners to review the regionalization schemes with explicit consideration of society's objectives.

Distribution of Income

Although income distribution is a very controversial subject,
ignoring this type of impact in the formulation of public investment
makes the model incomplete. It is important to distinguish between
changes on income distribution over time to a particular group and
redistribution within that particular group. This distinction makes
clearer the real distributional impacts of different investment activities under consideration in a national plan (Schmid 1972). Multiobjective methodology must be framed in this investment-opportunity
matrix to take into account, in one or more of its columns, the
distribution of project impacts in relation to the induced income
structure. This leads the decision maker to think about different
groups affected by a particular project or a set of projects (Kalter
and Stevens 1971); or, given the income structure of different groups
in society, to create the necessary mechanism to determine the
appropriate levels of capital flow to implement investment activities
which will be of benefit to a prespecified group in society (Haveman
1965).

The purpose of this section is not to theorize about income
distribution criteria or to discriminate between approaches. Rather,
the core of this section is to open the discussion to some distributional
aspects incorporated in certain projects. The distributional and
regional aspects of income generation are not independent, especially
if the regionalization criterion is one of delineating "pockets of
poverty."

Two elements may be introduced as qualifications of the level
of income as an attribute: distribution of output generated by the
project, and distribution of factor incomes generated by the invest-

ment. The former category explores the normative objective around "who" gets the output generated by a project. This is important when deciding about mutually exclusive types of projects (a liquor distillery versus a wheat milling industry). When one of the primary objectives of a society is to increase the standard of living of low-income people, and in particular their nutrition levels, the distribution of output patterns has to be taken into consideration.

For the latter elements the same criterion applies. The generated structure of salaries, wages, rent, interest, and other payments to factors is an important qualification of the level of income as an attribute of the IOM. Poverty lines, minimum factor's share, and other reference factors may all characterize different projects in the formulation process.

Attribute Two: Employment

This attribute is incorporated into the analysis of the IOM in recognition of an economic environment of the formulation model characterized by a labor surplus economy (UNIDO 1972). The number of people being employed by the investment plan is a critical variable to the real implementation of economic development. UNIDO (1972, p. 202) states that "the essence of surplus labor lies in the gap between the market wage in the organized, capitalistic sectors of the economy and the social value of the marginal product of labor in the rest of the economy . . . but in the traditional 'rest of the economy,' incomes are not in general determined by the rules of perfect competition."

Although in this book a one-type labor economy is assumed, it must be recognized that there are qualitative and quantitative differences in the types of labor. The labor may be classified as skilled and unskilled, or professional, craftsman, and operative labor (Haveman and Krutilla 1968). Second, dissemination is needed when different types of labor are incorporated in the analysis; this dissemination will be based upon the planners' most convenient way to identify their labor environment. Finally, if one attribute called "employment" is to be used (indexing by the use of principal component analysis or any other method), shadow pricing labor becomes a crucial factor.

This section of the chapter will first present a basic review of the theory of shadow prices of labor, then will state propositions on how to analytically incorporate a differential demand for labor, and finally will present some different dimensions of this attribute with measurement propositions.

Shadow Price of Labor

There is a commonly held notion that the social value of labor is represented by its product forgone from other activities in the economy as a result of the formulation and implementation of the investment plan. This notion, in a labor surplus economy, is put into operation by stating that the opportunity cost of labor is zero. In other words, a decrease in the amount of labor in the traditional sector will not diminish the final output of the sector. However, other refinements need to be analyzed. Harberger (1972) analyzed two basic notions related to the shadow price of labor: the zero marginal product, and the concept of supply price.

The agricultural sector in the economies of developing countries is the base in a family system of employment. In this type of system, the application of the idea of zero marginal physical product of labor becomes very attractive. Placing labor at a price equal to zero implicitly reflects that the labor absorbed from agriculture will not decrease the value of the agricultural product generated.

If the principle is that employers are not willing to pay more than the value of the marginal physical product of labor, this concept of zero shadow price weakens. As Harberger (1972, p. 82) states, this "hypothesis of zero shadow price was a 'straw man'." Reflections were made not only to the productivity of labor, but also the concept was reformulated taking into account the skill and seasonality associated with the aggregate demand for a particular type of labor. Harberger concluded, then, "that the best approximation to the marginal product of rural labor is the going market wage applicable to each skill category, and that the social opportunity cost of such labor, in the absence of substantial open unemployment, is also best measured by the going wage" (1972, p. 83).

Distinction has been made with respect to two main factors: employment in rural areas versus urban areas, and the probability of employing labor from areas of chronic unemployment. With respect to the first factor, the social opportunity cost of labor used to value labor employed in the rural areas is the going wage in the area, while those employed in the urban areas should be priced at the prevailing wage of the unprotected sector.

An extensive analysis was made by Haveman (1970) to evaluate the probability of absorbing people from pockets of unemployment. To assess the shadow price of labor, some steps have to be followed: (1) determine the patterns of demand imposed by a particular investment bundle for economic development; (2) compare these patterns of demand with the occupational patterns of labor unemployment and industrial patterns of excess capacity; and (3) determine a function to determine the real probability of getting labor absorbed from pockets of unemployment.

The concept of supply price assumes that a worker is free to decide at what wage bracket he/she would be willing to pass from unemployed to employed labor. In most of the cases this shadow price is not zero, as was the belief in the zero-marginal-product theory. If an unemployed worker is offered and accepts, for example, one dollar, the wage differential will be one dollar, and the traditional theory would predict that he/she would become employed. Empirical research has proven that this is not a realistic case.

Leaving aside for the moment the cultural patterns attached to employment behavior, an unemployed person should be paid at least a salary equal to his/her social value of leisure. This concept of leisure price, as the shadow price of unemployed labor, refines the concept of wage differential by stating that "the 'profit' which an unemployed worker makes upon getting a job is accordingly not the full wage, but the excess of that wage over his reservation price (supply price)" (Harberger 1972, p. 88).

UNIDO Shadow Price of Labor

UNIDO's "Guidelines for Project Evaluation" (1972) offers a shadow-price approach which takes into consideration three basic components: direct opportunity cost (z), indirect cost, and the redistribution of income. The direct cost of labor approach is similar to the product-forgone approach already discussed. The indirect cost relates essentially to how employment affects savings, especially employment of unemployed or very unskilled labor with a large marginal propensity to consume. To determine the shadow wage rate the following procedure is followed: It is first assumed that capital owners hired L units of labor at a given wage, w, which makes their net income equal to the gross income y minus $w \times L$; then an aggregate consumption value of the capital owners' annual income is defined per unit of investment I. Assuming the capital owners' propensity to save is s_k, the aggregate consumption will be

$$I \times s_k (y - wL) + (1 - s_k) (y - wL) \qquad (5.3)$$

If it is assumed that workers have a zero marginal propensity to save, the total worker consumption due to a marginal unit of investment is equal to $(w - z)L$. Then, total aggregate consumption will be

$$I \times s_k (y - wL) + (1 - s_k)(y - wL) + (w - z)L \qquad (5.4)$$

With these elements, a shadow-price-of-investment formula is derived given the social discount rate i:

$$I = \frac{I \times s_k (y - wL) + (1 - s_k)(y - wL) + (w - z)L}{i - s_k (y - wL)} \qquad (5.5)$$

where the expression $(1 - s_k)w$ measures the reduction in aggregate consumption, and $I \times s_k \times w$ measures the aggregate consumption value of the reduction in investment. Then, the indirect cost of employment is

$$[(1 - s_k) + (I \times s_k)]w - w = s_k (I - 1)w \qquad (5.6)$$

and the shadow wage rate, including the direct and indirect effects, is

$$w^* = z + s_k (I - 1)w \qquad (5.7)$$

If redistributional aspects have to be considered, the shadow wage rate becomes

$$w^{**} = w^* + v [z + (s_k p_w - 1)w] \qquad (5.8)$$

where p_w represents the present value of worker's foregone consumption, and v represents a redistributional weight. UNIDO (1972) introduced other refinements into this shadow wage rate following the same analytical patterns.

All these shadow pricing approaches have assumed that an optimal balance has been reached between different objectives of the economy (income, foreign exchange, redistribution). At the formulation stage this is not necessarily the case.

In this multiple-objective framework, we will use units of labor employed by different investment projects. For simplicity, a one-type of labor economy will be assumed; but this assumption is easily taken out of the analysis.

In a two-objective society (employment and income), the social price of labor will be directly related to how society evaluates its welfare level when one additional unit of labor is employed. It is a merit-want concept rather than a marginal concept of shadow wage rate. Given the weights attached by society to employment and income (welfare function), the shadow wage rate will be determined by the slope of the established feasibility frontier (different trade-offs between income and employment).

As will be seen later, the multiobjective technique used here will enable the planners to characterize attributes in totally different units of measurement. The column in the investment-opportunity matrix will contain the number of people employed by different projects who were unemployed before. This is an idea of net absorption of employment. The direction of preferences in labor surplus economies will favor those projects with a large absorption of labor.

Attribute Three: Foreign Exchange

This attribute is incorporated into the decision model in recognition of foreign exchange as a very scarce resource in developing countries. Foreign exchange has frequently been used as an important attribute of a multiobjective decision-making framework.*

Little and Mirrlees (1974, p. 43) state that "it is often said that two of the basic shortages facing developing countries are foreign exchange and savings. . . . Foreign exchange is a scarce resource like any other."

The output of a particular project generates foreign exchange by substituting for imports, and by permitting greater exporting to the world market. Moreover, taking into consideration different projects, associated to each investment bundle will be a certain flow of foreign exchange which often allows governments in developing countries to close the foreign-trade balance gap.

Because a project may generate several different types of foreign exchange (dollars, pesos, marks, pounds, yen), it is important to analyze some of the approaches dealing with shadow pricing these hard currencies from the developing country's point of view. Also, some criteria and rules for ranking projects based on their foreign exchange composition (taking into consideration that most developing countries are export economies) will be presented briefly.

Shadow Price of Foreign Exchange†

Three basic criteria may be used to shadow price foreign exchange: (1) shadow price will reflect in value terms the increase in welfare of the economy as a result of a one-unit increase in foreign exchange; (2) shadow price should reflect the opportunity cost of the foreign exchange in alternative uses; and (3) shadow price should reflect, in a way, the "equilibrium" exchange rate.

---

*Avramovic (1958 and 1964), Bhagwati (1970), Balassa (1964), Davis (1959), UNIDO (1972), Little and Mirrlees (1974).

†This section will rely heavily upon Bacha and Taylor (1972), UNIDO (1972), and Little and Mirrlees (1974).

The Welfare Approach

Assuming that the economy is in equilibrium, a project which generates or uses foreign exchange will produce a displacement of the economy to a different welfare state. Two main welfare models will be presented here: the Programming Model and the Harberger-Schydlowsky-Fontaine Model. The first one focuses particularly on the basic activities which will induce a reevaluation of the foreign exchange rate: activities associated with restriction to foreign trade (tariffs, protections, quotas); different bottlenecks of the economy which are results of a structural dependency on foreign-type goods; and government activities related to foreign exchange rate policies.

The Harberger-Schydlowsky-Fontaine Model attempts to determine a shadow price based on a concept of an export economy in which there are three main sectors: import-competing sector, export sector, and domestic sector. The actual shadow pricing will result from an interaction of these sectors' supplies and demands for foreign exchange, assuming a system of floating exchange rates.

The Opportunity-Cost Approach

This approach has a very direct relationship with the next section (efficiency) and will be presented then.

The "Equilibrium" Approach

The shadow price of foreign exchange is a value which results from the equilibrium between its supply and demand; the equilibrium exchange rate. Bacha and Taylor (1972, p. 47) "define the equilibrium exchange rate as that which prevails in a floating foreign exchange market when all import restrictions and export subsidies are removed."

Besides this equilibrium exchange rate, the parity exchange rate is also considered as a shadow price: "Purchasing power parity exchange rates are alternatively defined as (i) the exchange rate between two currencies that equates the market value of a representative basket of final goods in the two countries, or (ii) the rate that reestablishes the real value of a country's official exchange rate as measured from a given base year by use of a general price index" (Bacha and Taylor 1972, p. 51).

UNIDO Approach

UNIDO (1972, p. 216) defines the shadow price of foreign exchange as "a weighted average of the ratios of market-clearing to official c.i.f. prices, the weights reflecting the content of the marginal import bill." UNIDO also considers two main concepts of this shadow price depending upon, first, if it represents a pure equilibrium rate, and second, if foreign exchange represents a merit want (programming approach). The definition given in the previous paragraph answers the question: "Given the level and composition of imports and exports, either actual or prospective, what is (will be) the value in domestic terms of the goods that a marginal unit of foreign exchange would make available?" (UNIDO 1972, p. 224).

However, once again this definition assumes that an optimal balance has been reached between different objectives of the economy—consumption, income, employment, redistribution. This introduces the actual meaning that the foreign exchange will have in this model: assuming two objectives (employment and foreign exchange), the foreign exchange shadow price will be the result of a trade-off between these two objectives, in other words, the slope of an existent feasibility frontier between these objectives.

This particular definition touches upon the welfare approach analyzed before:

> In principle, it may be possible to elicit from policy
> makers in advance of project formulation and evaluation
> the weight, W^F, to be placed on foreign exchange, con-
> sidered as a merit want. . . . Just as choice between
> alternative water-distribution schemes would reveal a
> range of weights on the benefits of poor peasants relative
> to aggregate-consumption benefits . . . and choice
> between alternative techniques of irrigation would reveal
> a range of social discount rates . . . so would the choice
> among alternatives that differ with respect to their
> impact on foreign and domestic resources reveal the
> range in which the weight of foreign exchange implicit
> in the choice between these alternatives lies (UNIDO
> 1972, p. 228).

This is the approach taken here. The vein of the argument will be picked up in the last part of this section.

Foreign Exchange and Investment Criteria

The opportunity-cost approach allows one to introduce some criteria which are based upon the foreign-exchange component of different investment activities. Projects may be compared and also ranked, based upon their intrinsic costs of generating one unit of foreign exchange. This relates to the value added of each of the projects under consideration, and then to the concept of rate of effective protection. No discussion will be presented of this concept although there is a relation.

Bruno (1972) developed formulas that relate to the definition of benefit and to what is called domestic resource cost; the opportunity cost of generating one unit of foreign exchange. He states that benefits, B_j, can be separated into two types: those related to tradable goods of a project, and those associated with nontradable goods (including different factors of production). This benefit, B_j, as a rule, will be used to accept projects whose B_j are greater than zero and reject those whose B_j are less than zero.

Domestic resource cost, d_j, was defined as the ratio between B_j and the net foreign exchange earned or saved. It is an index which reflects the social cost of effective protection. Bruno (1972) proves that, given an accounting rate of exchange, d_o, the rule $B_j \gtreqless 0$ is equivalent to a rule $d_j \lesseqgtr d_o$. He concluded that the rate of effective protection is equivalent to the domestic resource cost concept when all goods of the project are tradable.

Krueger (1972) also offers a formula for representing the domestic-resource-cost criterion, which is essentially the opportunity cost of factors of production to a per-unit dollar net of international value added and repatriation expenses in a particular project.

Net Generation of Foreign Exchange

These different opportunity costs of foreign exchanges will allow planners to fill the columns relating to foreign exchange. These columns will account for the net generation of foreign exchange and for the planning period (year-by-year basis) of each of the projects under consideration. This figure represents a combined demand for foreign inputs and a supply of tradable output. This attribute will set differences between projects with a large component of foreign inputs and nontradable goods to other projects with a large proportion of tradable goods and a small component of foreign inputs.

Under a situation of foreign exchange scarcity, the direction of preferences favors those projects whose net contributions are higher.

SOURCE-OF-FUNDS MATRIX

The characterization of the IOM and its main features can be applied directly to the SOFM. In particular, some of the attributes which will characterize each of the sources of funds will be examined. Other attributes may be introduced into the analysis depending upon the problem and the availability of data.

There are two ways of classifying different sources of funds:
functional and statistical (Mikesell 1964). The functional classification of loans involves the following categories: (1) long-term loans
for financing specific investment programs; (2) long-term loans for
general use, or balance-of-payments purposes not attributed to
specific projects; (3) loans by development banks to developing countries; (4) loans which will perform the role of monetary stabilization;
(5) loans for financing specific exports needed by the donor country;
(6) loans for financing the production of strategic commodities
(weapons); and (7) loans with the purpose of stimulating foreign
private investment in regions of the world which are characterized
by insufficient economic growth (Mikesell 1964).

The statistical classification of loans is not concerned with the
purposes of a particular loan; rather it characterizes a loan by its
attributes or potential impact on the recipient country. The loans
are classified by their interest rate, grace period, maturity, or
any other relevant attribute. Based on these attributes, government
will base its priorities on different loans, under the assumption that
it can adequately allocate these financial resources for economic
development.

The SOFM is constructed using the statistical classification of
the loans, and this becomes a key element of the decision model.

The Effective Interest Rate

The effective interest rate is related to the concept of "real
capacity" of generating foreign exchange. Also, it relates to the
real value of a loan to the recipient country. The higher the interest
rate the "harder" the loan, and the more money has to be compro-
mised in the future to repay a specific loan. Conversely, the lower
the effective interest rate the more convenient the loan is, other
things being equal.

The mathematical formula that will measure this attribute will
depend upon the definition of effective interest rate adopted. The
one related to the real cost of generating foreign currencies for
repayment purposes is given by Fontaine and Selowsky (1972). They
used this formula to calculate the effective interest rate of Inter-
American Development Bank Agency for International Development,
International Bank for Reconstruction and Development, and Exim-
bank loans during the period 1961 to 1970.

The effective interest rate, r, is the rate that equates the following expression:

$$O_t = NF_t + NF_{t-1}(1 + r) + \ldots + NF_{t-n-1}(1 + r)^{n-1} +$$

$$O_{t-n}(1 + r)^n \qquad (5.9)$$

where O_t represents the debt at the end of period t, NF_t represents the financial flows during period t (payments minus amortization plus interest and commissions), and O_{t-n} represents the debt at the beginning of the period t - n.

For the other concept of effectiveness, a proportionality index may be used, in particular, the proportion between the nominal interest rate and the value of the loan discounted by the cost due to tieing.

The representative formula is

$$i^* = \frac{i}{C \times F} \times 100 \qquad\qquad (5.10)$$

where i represents the nominal interest rate, C the estimated cost of a tied loan,* and F the face value of the loan.

Maturity, Grace, and Amortization

These three attributes are found directly in the loan's contract and are measured in years. Of particular importance in the short run is the grace period: that period (in years) in which the country pays only the interest. It is found in this contract that, in general, there are two interest rates: one associated with the grace period and the other with the aftergrace period.

The tied portion of a loan represents another attribute that is taken into consideration in determining the real benefits of one unit of loan flow to the recipient country. Two basic arguments are stated against tied loans: they produce trade-diversion effects, and they exert a potential degree of monopoly power exercised by the donor.

An index frequently used in classifying loans is the degree of tiedness: that proportion which the tied portion of the loan represents in the total face value of the loan.

Cost of Debt

The cost of debt represents an index used by businessmen in calculating a rough cost of different loans. This cost-of-debt index is represented by the ratio between total interest paid and the principal of the loan.

———

*UNCTAD estimated that it is around 20-30 percent, see Frank (1970).

Subsidy Element of a Loan

This attribute is also called the grant element or concessional value of a loan. The basic objective is to measure how much of the given loan represents a real subsidy to the recipient when compared with its real opportunity cost.

The calculations may be modified depending upon the specific type of contract that is being signed.

The following terms will be used to define the subsidy element of a loan:

i_{t-G} the interest rate of the loan after the grace period

i_G the interest rate of the loan before the grace period

r   discount rate

G   grace period

T   maturity

F   face value of the loan

P   total present value of future payments at time of lending

GE   grant element of the loan (F-P)

ge   GE/F

The interest payment during the grace period, G, will be represented by

$$PV_1 = \sum_0^G \frac{i_G \times F}{(1 + r)^G}$$

(5.11)

After the grace period, in which only interest is paid, the remaining portion of the principal will be repaid at a rate equal to 1/T - G.

The present value formula that determines the discounted value after the grace period is

$$PV_2 = \sum_{t=G}^T \frac{F/T - G}{(1 + r)^t} + \left| \frac{i_{t-G} \, (F - F\frac{t - G}{T - G})}{(1 + r)^t} \right|$$

(5.12)

The total present value of this loan at the appropriate discount rate is equal to the sum of PV_1 and PV_2.

$$PV = PV_1 + PV_2$$

(5.13)

In equation 5.12 we have two general components: a proportional payment of the principal, and a payment of interest accumulated from the unpaid balance.

Other Indicators

As other examples of statistical characterization of loans, three other attributes will be considered: dependency, concentration, and probability of getting the loan. A dependency indicator will capture the percentage of the total face value of the loan that is tied to the donor—the trade diversion effects. The concentration indicator is a measure of market control exercised in the source from which the loan is contracted. In particular, a measure may be the number of developing countries that are receiving a loan from the particular source of funds (country). The probability of getting a loan is here measured by the amount of total lending by a particular source of funds as compared with the GNP of that source; we measure the lending "capacity" of the source of funds.

SUMMARY

The general objectives of the economy—representing a state toward which planners hope the economy is proceeding—give the basic criteria for determining the general investment goals. As emphasized earlier, these goals are implemented in a context of competitive use for resources, and the trade-offs would be assessed at different stages of development planning. In Chapter 2 special reference was made to the organizational structure and the different steps of investment planning decisions in the context of public choices and the different parts of the decision system proposed by implementation of the decision-making model.

The need for a uniform method of determining priorities at the formulation level requires a cause-effect informational structure. This structure must reflect the real contributions of each investment activity to the accomplishment of society's goals. The structure is composed of two matrixes: investment-opportunities, and source-of-funds.

The array of projects represented by the rows of the investment-opportunity matrix is characterized by a multiplicity of objectives. Four attributes, representing those objectives, were analyzed: income, employment, foreign exchange, and net present value. The conceptual definitions of each of these attributes set the basic framework to determine the contribution by each project to the developmental needs of a particular country. This setting may be applied ex ante and ex post to the evaluation stage.

Putting these concepts into a specific index or formula will be functionally dependent upon the quality and availability of data. Once the model is found useful by planning agencies, they would be willing to generate the required informational flows to implement the model.

The second part of this chapter dealt with the basic elaborations to characterize different sources of funds by their statistical attributes. Because of early developments of financial analysis, some of these attributes are easy to implement. This made it possible to offer more specific formulas and reduced-form indexes to incorporate in the source-of-funds matrix.

In concluding this chapter, it should be emphasized that the IOM and SOFM were presented here in a primarily heuristic setting. That is, the main purpose has been to illustrate the concept of an IOM and a SOFM rather than to focus unduly on the elements of these two matrixes. The analysis performed in Chapters 7 and 8 will employ data for a hypothetical decision process with the principal aim of illustrating the usefulness of goal programming in developing country decision making. Before turning to these examples, however, it is necessary to devote some attention to the economics of financial management for an optimally constituted investment program; this is the subject of Chapter 6.

REFERENCES

Avramovic, Dragoslav. 1958. Debt Service Capacity and Postwar Growth in International Indebtedness. Baltimore: Johns Hopkins University Press.

Bacha, E., and L. Taylor. 1972. "Foreign-Exchange Shadow Prices: A Critical Review of Current Theories." In Benefit-Cost Analysis: 1971, ed. A. C. Harberger. Chicago: Aldine-Atherton.

Balassa, Bela. 1964. "The Capital Needs of the Developing Countries." Kyklos 18, no. 2: 197-206.

Bhagwati, Jagdish. 1970. International Trade. Baltimore: Penguin Books.

Bruno, Michael. 1972. "Domestic Resource Cost and Effective Protection: Clarification and Synthesis." Journal of Political Economy 80, no. 1 (January-February): 16-32.

Davis, John H. 1959. "Agricultural Surpluses and Foreign Aid." American Economic Review Papers and Proceedings 49, no. 2 (May): 232-41.

Fisher, I. 1969. "Income and Capital." In Readings in the Concept and Measurement of Income, ed. R. H. Parker and G. C. Harcourt. Cambridge: Cambridge University Press, pp. 33-53.

Fontaine, Ernesto, and Marcelo Selowsky. 1972. "Algunas Consideraciones Sobre el Financiamiento Externo en un Contexto de Costos y Beneficios." Revista de Economia 9, no. 28 (December) (Universidad Catolica de Chile).

Frank, C. R. 1970. Debt and Terms of Aid. Overseas Development Council, Monograph No. 1.

Harberger, Arnold C. 1972. "On Measuring the Social Opportunity Cost of Labor." In Benefit-Cost Analysis, 1971, ed. A. Harberger. Chicago: Aldine-Atherton.

Haveman, Robert H. 1965. Water Resource Investment and the Public Interest. Nashville, Tenn.: Vanderbilt University Press.

____. 1970. "Evaluating Public Expenditures Under Conditions of Unemployment." In Public Expenditure and Policy Analysis, ed. R. Haveman and J. Margolis. Chicago: Rand McNally.

Haveman, Robert H., and John V. Krutilla. 1968. Unemployment, Idle Capacity, and the Evaluation of Public Expenditures: National and Regional Analysis. Baltimore: Johns Hopkins University Press.

Hicks, J. R. 1969. "Income." In Readings in the Concept and Measurement of Income, ed. R. H. Parker and G. C. Harcourt. Cambridge: Cambridge University Press, pp. 74-82.

Kalter, R. J., and T. H. Stevens. 1971. "Resource Investments, Impact Distribution, and Evaluation Concepts." American Journal of Agricultural Economics 53, no. 2 (May): 206-15.

Krueger, Anne. 1972. "Evaluating Restrictionist Trade Regimes: Theory and Measurement." Journal of Political Economy 80, no. 1 (January-February): 48-61.

Lindahl, E. 1969. "The Concept of Income." In Readings in the Concept and Measurement of Income, ed. R. H. Parker and G. C. Harcourt. Cambridge: Cambridge University Press, pp. 54-62.

Little, I. M. D., and J. A. Mirrlees. 1974. Project Appraisal
   and Planning for Development Countries. New York: Basic
   Books.

Mikesell, Raymond F. 1964. Mecanismos de Ayuda Economica
   Externa. Mexico City: Estudios CEMLA.

Morrison, D. F. 1967. Multivariate Statistical Methods. New York:
   McGraw-Hill.

Schmid, A. Allan. 1972. "Changed Distribution of Income vs.
   Redistribution in Public Project Evaluation." American Journal
   of Agricultural Economics 54 (February): 135-36.

Simons, H. C. 1969. "The Definition of Income." In Readings in
   the Concept and Measurement of Income, ed. R. H. Parker and
   G. C. Harcourt. Cambridge: Cambridge University Press,
   pp. 63-73.

UNIDO. 1972. Guidelines for Project Evaluation. New York: United
   Nations Industrial Development Organization.

Waterston, Albert. 1974. "The Coming Surge in Regional Planning."
   Finance and Development 2, no. 2.

CHAPTER

6

THE ECONOMICS
OF PROJECT FINANCING

The increasing importance of foreign trade, international financial obligations, and foreign debt in developing countries raises new questions about one very crucial aspect of investment planning, that of project financing and foreign debt management. As the composition of developing country investments changes, it becomes increasingly crucial to conduct careful analyses of the sources of developing country borrowing, of the mix of domestic and foreign currency generated by investments, and of the sequencing of project components. Much of the literature on project evaluation ignores these crucial elements in developing country decision making. The purpose of this chapter is to seek some analytical criteria for external financing based on each project's ability to generate foreign exchange. This approach is developed under the assumption that the market for foreign exchange is economically and institutionally imperfect; a recipient country can change foreign currency for domestic currency but not domestic for foreign currency, and the transfer from foreign-exchange surplus to deficit activities is limited. In this context we find the government acting as a central economic unit which invests in an optimal program—optimal investment strategy—and then must repay the loan to different sources of finance. Self-sustained development policies must be designed to reckon with this structural imperfection and thus it is necessary to develop criteria to optimally allocate different sources of funds to individual projects.

These imperfections may be the result of many economic, social, and institutional factors which will force the government to implement high social-cost activities. For example, a law which prohibits transfers of pesos into dollars: it may reflect an economic state characterized by many low-income individuals who do not produce savings to be transferred into dollars; or there may be other structural bottlenecks in the economy. Given these factors, the financing of a project in dollars without careful attention to its capacity to generate foreign exchange will force the government to promote exports, sacrifice imports, redistribute income, and so on; actions which are not socially costless.

A graphic description of our framework is presented in Figure 6.1. The same assumptions used in developing the investment decision model apply here, particularly the one that refers to projects which are large compared to national income.

The initial presentation of the programming methodology included as part of its constraints aggregates cost and budget availability to finance the proposed development plans and we did not deal with a distinguishable budget. Here, these aspects of financing are rather more complex because of the double (or multiple) tier cost structure—foreign and domestic borrowing—and the direct impacts upon the balance of payments in developing countries. Concerning the effect upon the balance of payments, we characterized projects from the output side by making both the qualitative and quantitative distinction of the foreign exchange contribution by each project to economic development. However, there is another characterization of projects: as generators of currencies particularly relevant to the repayment capacity of developing economies. It is this second characterization which concerns us in this chapter.

It was long ago recognized that an increased capital stock held important implications for the manner and degree to which this stock would have to be financed by foreign borrowings.* This is based upon the multiplier theory and the absorption approach to the balance of payments. The argument is as follows: Increases in the capital stock of the economy—the financing of new projects—would increase income levels in the economy. But, because of a marginal propensity to import greater than zero, income increases will increase imports and deteriorate the balance of payments. The availability of foreign borrowings would supposedly alleviate these pressures by enlarging domestic savings and diminishing the time required to achieve a given stage of growth. In spite of these potential beneficial effects, the basic question remained: how do planners allocate foreign capital to alternative domestic investments?

Polak (1950) presented a rule of thumb that would help developing countries to make these allocative decisions. The rule consisted of

---

*We can only partially review the relevant literature here because of its scope. Emphasis will be on those aspects which relate capital investment with domestic versus foreign borrowings. See Polak (1950), Buchanan (1945), Kahn (1951), Chenery (1953), Lombardini (1969), and others.

FIGURE 6.1

The Financing Process

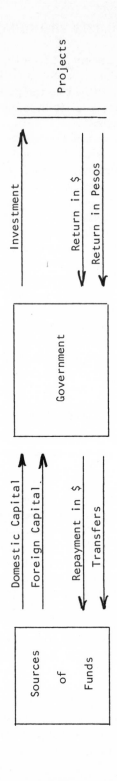

Source: Compiled by the authors.

classifying potentially available investments by their major type of commodity in relation to foreign trade. He characterized Type I investments as those projects which will directly contribute to foreign exchange earnings: export and import substituting industries. Type II projects were considered neutral to foreign exchange flows: replacement investments for foreign or domestically sold commodities. Finally, Type III projects were those which, given the foreign trade multiplier, would worsen the balance of payments. Examples are investments in domestic projects, such as highways, which would raise domestic incomes and so imports. For a given amount of foreign aid available, the financial criteria which would favor the balance of payments in the long run was twofold: to favor Type I investments, and, within this type of project, to choose those of highest output/capital turnover ratio (Q/K). Using this criterion, countries would maximize their welfare and reduce foreign dependency.

Kahn (1951) and Chenery (1953) raised several problems with this approach. First, there is the assumption of a positive correlation between Q/K, the investment turnover ratio, and the contribution to the balance of payments. Chenery was able to demonstrate that, in some cases, there may be a negative correlation between these two effects so that attention must be paid to both simultaneously.* Second, in the context of developing countries, their large marginal propensity to import implies that financing investment with foreign or domestic savings would always accentuate this circle of foreign debt. This is particularly important since the first stage of development in developing countries generally encompasses Type III investments with a very low rate of capital turnover.

---

*Chenery rationalized this criterion by defining the social marginal product of projects (SMP), or the marginal rate of substitution between national income and the balance of payment (net) as SMP = $\Delta V = \Delta Y + r \Delta B$ where: ΔY = income effects and ΔB = balance-of-payments effect. This equation may be expanded by taking into account incremental capital K; social value added domestically $V = X + E - M_i$ (where E is added value of output due to external economies, M_i the cost of imported materials, and X is increased value of output); and total cost of domestic factors $C = L + Md + O$ (where L is labor cost, Md is cost of domestic material, and O overhead cost). This equation will then be: SMP = $V/K - C/K + \frac{Br}{K}$ or SMP = $V/K \left(\frac{V - C}{K}\right) + Br/K$ where V/K is capital turnover, C/K is the cost ratio, Br/K the balance-of-payments effect, and $\frac{V - C}{V}$ the value margin. For more details see Chenery (1953).

Neither the Chenery-Kahn approach nor recent developments in the literature have solved the problem of defining an optimal trade-off between foreign and domestic currencies to finance individual projects. Chenery's proposition did not answer the question of how related were the profitability (SMP), real needs for foreign financing, and possibilities of repayment. The balance-of-payments impacts depend only in part on the potential inflows (or "transfer" effect of foreign borrowing); it is also necessary to consider the time, pattern, and schedule of debt repayment; there is a natural limit imposed by the decrease in purchasing power at time of repayment. In developing countries this problem is often of particular importance because of the significant burden imposed by foreign debt.

Also, there is a constraint because the currency mix for project financing usually consists of a very large component in foreign borrowings–dollars–compared to a very weak domestic currency–say, pesos. In essence, the literature has not resolved the problem of repayment capacity at the project level. One of the reasons is that it has been assumed that there is a transfer mechanism of pesos to dollars from the surplus dollar-producing activities to the deficit ones; a well-functioning structure or allocative mechanism that will transfer, in an almost perfect manner, different units of foreign and domestic exchange. This assumed transfer mechanism may take place among different projects, between projects and other sectors of the economy, or among different sectors of the economy.

To facilitate the presentation of the financial model we have assumed that we are considering an economy with an extreme institutional imperfection in the foreign–domestic currency markets such that ready exchange of, say, pesos into dollars cannot take place. The traditional approach considers the transformation of foreign currency generated or absorbed by a particular project as a straightforward application of the appropriate shadow foreign-exchange rate. The next section will present a more realistic financial model for investment decisions in developing countries. The presentation considers four aspects: (1) the model; (2) the optimal currency mix for project financing under assumptions that repayment capacity must be framed at the project level; (3) foreign aid management which enables countries, once total foreign aid requirements are determined, to find the most convenient sources; and (4) disbursement so that once the funds are available for the project, the sequencing of project components is carried out in an optimal fashion.

The aim of this chapter will be to explore these problems and offer some policy alternatives. The chapter, as with the others, will be primarily methodological, with the presentation of some specific examples to better illustrate the analysis.

THE METHOD

The financial model, which is part of the total investment decision model presented in Chapter 2, deals with three main decisions: (1) what is the optimal mix between foreign and domestic currency; (2) from which foreign sources should funds be obtained; and (3) once funds are available, what is the optimal disbursement policy. The model is graphically presented in Figure 6.2. It is an interactive part of the investment formulation model, particularly that part which refers to the financial aspects of project selection.

The financial model considers two decision-making levels. The first is mainly concerned with determining the investment structure of projects. Assuming a two-currency world of pesos and dollars, the model will determine the optimal currency mix for each project as a function of its foreign-exchange-producing capacity in isolation from others. With the optimal investment increment to the economy's capital stock (X^*) known, the model will determine the optimal foreign and domestic currency requirements of the investment plan. The second level of decision making considers all the potential sources of funds of the foreign currency, in our example dollars. These sources $(S_1, S_2, \ldots, S_n)$ are then characterized by their statistical attributes (interest rate, grace period, maturity, and the like) which then form the source-of-funds matrix of the goal programming model. Assuming a welfare function for the decision maker similar to the one used in the project selection process,* the model will provide the policy maker with an "ideal" ranking or preference vector based on the statistical attributes of the foreign sources of funds. Once the planning agencies possess the financial means to implement development projects, the final task is to explore ways and means to optimally disburse the funds: optimally in the sense that the manner and degree in which disbursement is realized will always maximize the project's objectives. Put somewhat differently, different ways of disbursing available financial resources and different ways of implementing projects result in fundamentally different projects.

OPTIMAL CURRENCY MIX

In this section it will be assumed that the individual projects represent new economic units in a system in which transfer of pesos

---

*In this case we have assumed a given set of goals which would reflect the decision maker's preferences over the attributes (characteristics) of different foreign sources; for example, g corresponding to the interest rate might be considered zero.

FIGURE 6.2

The Economics of Project Financing

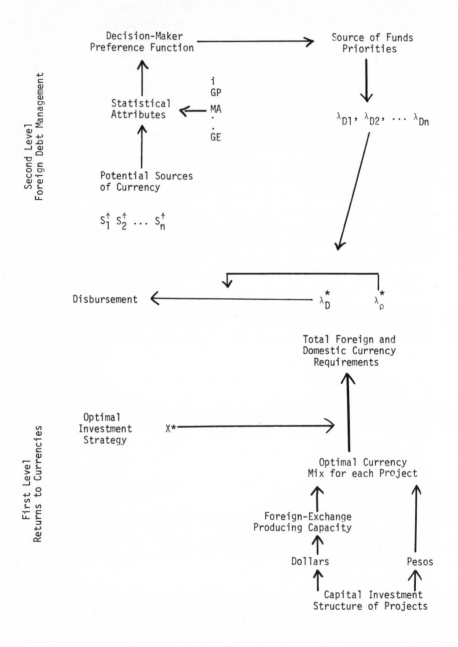

to dollars is not possible. Under this condition a model will be developed which would provide the economist/planner with the optimal proportion of dollars to pesos to finance these projects. At the end of this section we will discuss the major implications of holding a "nontransferability" assumption, and we will offer some analytical alternatives if it is relaxed. The procedure in this section first considers the determination of a formula to ascertain the optimal currency mix for a hypothetical project. Then the formula is generalized for n projects. Finally, based on the initial formulation, assessment will be made of the optimal investment bundle's demand for foreign borrowings.

One of the important aspects of this problem area is that in many projects the proportion of borrowed foreign currency attached to them is not responsive to a set of basic economic variables. Consider, for example, that a country—under the assumption of nontransferability—would like to generate its repayment capacity at the project level. It is immediately evident that if the project, per unit of capital investment, has a high internal rate at which it generates dollars as compared with its ability to generate pesos, the proportion of dollars to pesos should be larger in financing the capital structure of such a project (export-producing or import-substituting projects), ceteris paribus. Moreover, if the cost of foreign borrowing increases, other things equal, the proportion of dollars to pesos must go down. Finally, if the opportunity cost of a peso goes up relative to the dollar (the dollar becomes cheaper), the proportion of pesos must go down, ceteris paribus. These are elements which must be taken into consideration in deciding the optimal capital structure of a development project.

Optimal Financial Structure:
Two Sources of Funds

It is important to state at the outset that the optimal currency mix will be calculated for the "uncommitted" capital flows of the project (UKP): that portion of the capital investment of the project that is not tied to a specific currency. The economist/planner may be able to determine those project components that must be financed in dollars or pesos regardless of their potential capital structure. In this section we assume that all the capital investment of the project is subject to adjustment for optimal currency mix.

To illustrate this problem we begin by assuming a hypothetical project whose cash flows, in pesos and dollars, are described in Table 6.1. The rows in this table represent different types of cash flows, gross and net of repayments. The first six columns represent

TABLE 6.1

Hypothetical Project Cash Flows and Loan Repayment Schedule
(foreign exchange rate)

CASH FLOW \ YEAR	1	2	3	4	5	6	INTERNAL RATE OF RETURN	
(1) Pesos	500	400	400	300	200	200	30% :	IRR^P
(2) Dollars	100	200	300	400	500	600	20% :	$IRR^\$$
(3) Total	600	600	700	700	700	800	60% :	IRR^T
(4) Repayment Schedule	0	200	200	200	200	200		
(5) Dollars net of Repayment	100	0	100	200	300	400	2.5% :	$IRR^\$_N$
(6) Total Net of Repayment	600	400	500	500	500	600	46.5% :	IRR^T_N

* Foreign Exchange Rate

₱ = 1

Cost of the Project 100

*Assume: Foreign Exchange Rate of P = 1 and Project Cost of 100.

<u>Source:</u> Compiled by the authors.

the years of the project economic life considered for the analysis.
Under these conditions of highly distinguishable cash flows,* the
economist/planner must consider a set of internal rates of return
for the (1) cash flow in pesos; (2) cash flow in dollars; (3) total cash
flow; (4) cash flow in dollars net of repayment; and (5) total cash
flow net of repayment. These are presented in the last column of
Table 6.1.

For illustration it has been assumed that the interest rate on
foreign borrowing is 7.75 percent, and that the accounting rate of
exchange in this two-currency world is initially equal to 1 (ρ).

In the traditional analysis which assumes a world of perfect
currency transferability—among the project's activities, the project
and sectors, and among sectors of the economy—the relevant rate
of return is the IRR_N^T (total net of repayment) which, for this project,
is 46.5 percent. This rate of return is greater than the borrowing
rate of 7.75 percent, with the conclusion being that a financing in
dollars of the project will potentially increase the borrowing country's
welfare.

This analysis does not apply under conditions of nontransferability. The real economic state of the project calls for a qualitative
and quantitative distinction between cash flows of both currencies.†
In particular, the internal rate of return to dollar cash flows, net
of repayment, is only 2.5 percent. If it is impossible to convert
pesos into dollars, also net of repayment, there is a net social cost
of financing represented by the difference between the borrowing
rate of 7.75 percent and $IRR_N^\$$ of 2.5 percent. If the dollar cash
flow, net of repayment, is discounted at a rate of 7.75 percent,
there is a net loss for society of $217 which must be generated else-
where to help cancel the foreign debt.

We will refer again to the relevancy of this social cost of financing. For the moment, under circumstances that do not allow

------

*These are direct and indirect net financial cash flows (benefits
minus costs). In the case of cash flows in dollars we take into account
direct sales to foreign markets, substitution of imports, and all
foreign-exchange-producing activities. By the same token, cash
flows in pesos are all the activities of the project which do not generate foreign exchange.

†The reader may remember at this stage our discussion about
the "domestic resource cost" criterion. In considering foreign
exchange as a limiting resource for economic development, Bruno-
Krueger-Balassa separated the project's cash flows into domestic
and foreign, and based on this distinction they developed the DRC
criterion. We are establishing the same base for the financial flows
of the hypothetical project.

conversion of surplus peso into dollars among project activities, this $217 must be generated (and transferred abroad) from elsewhere in the domestic economy, otherwise, the country must borrow from abroad and/or further increase its foreign debt. In economies plagued by a severe foreign exchange shortage—as is the case for a majority of developing countries—this implies a decrease in imports, the promotion of exports, or very restrictive foreign trade policies, all of which may have a very high social cost.

The analytical framework to determine a criterion for the optimal currency mix in financing a project is based upon minimizing the total average cost of capital subject to the project's capacity to produce an extra unit of domestic and foreign currency.* The first-order condition of this constrained minimization problem indicates that the ratio of the cost of the loan (c) to the opportunity cost of capital in the borrowing country (k) must equal the ratio of marginal physical products of the currencies weighted by their proportional mix. This may be expressed as:

$$\frac{c}{k} = \frac{\alpha \text{IRR}^{\$}_{N}}{(1 - \alpha)\ \text{IRR}^{T}_{N} \times \rho} \tag{6.1}$$

where the IRRs represent the physical/financial productivity of each currency in the project. For two sources of funds the proportion (α) that should be financed in pesos can be calculated as:

$$\alpha = \frac{1}{\dfrac{k\text{IRR}^{\$}_{N}}{c\text{IRR}^{T}_{N} \times \rho} + 1} \tag{6.2}$$

With this formulation, we can observe that, ceteris paribus, (1) the higher the opportunity cost of capital in the borrowing country (k) the lower the proportion financed in domestic currency; (2) the higher the cost of borrowing abroad (c) the greater the proportion financed in domestic currency; (3) the higher the internal rate of

---

*One way of looking at a project is to frame its benefit and costs over time. In this particular case we are concerned about its financial flows by assuming that a project is a producer of currencies, in this case, pesos and dollars. We have assumed that the objective here is to minimize the total average cost of capital of the project, subject to technical characteristics of the "production function."

return of foreign currency cash flows ($IRR^{\$}_N$) the lower the proportion financed with the domestic currency; and (4) the higher the internal rate of return of domestic currency flows ($IRR^T_N \times \rho$) the larger the proportion financed with domestic currency.

The formula can be simplified to generalize for a case of n sources of funds. The optimality relation implies that for any two sources i and j:

$$\frac{\alpha_i}{\alpha_j} = \frac{c_j \rho_j IRR^i}{c_i \rho_i IRR^j} \tag{6.3}$$

and

$$\sum_{i,j} \alpha_i = 1 \tag{6.4}$$

where c_i represents the financial/social cost of source i (similarly for c_j), ρ_i represents units of domestic currency to foreign currency i (similarly for ρ_j), and IRR^i represents the internal rate of return of flows in currency i (similarly for currency j).

In private firms the cash flows—the base for the determination of IRRs—may be quantified in pure financial terms; the project borrowing and repayment capacity would not compromise other resources of the economic unit. However, public investments also account for social, indirect, and unquantifiable benefits and costs. Although the concept of a project so far has been purely financial (for repayment purposes) the inclusion of items in the different currencies' general cash flows will depend on the planner's judgment. This judgment must reflect the basic principles of repayment capacity applied in the country's economic, institutional, and social framework.

A Comment on the Proposed Criterion

First, the formulas presented above respond to a linear objective function and it has been assumed that the foreign exchange rate is constant. The total weighted cost-of-capital function has been assumed to be linear, though it need not be; it may take logarithmic or exponential forms. Also, we have assumed the foreign exchange rate as a parameter rather than a variable; there are some cases in which the amount of dollars is a function of the foreign exchange rate, or changes in the foreign exchange rate might produce continuous changes in the dollar/pesos cash flow composition. In particular, changes in the foreign exchange rate may change the allocation of resources between the tradable and nontradable goods produced or consumed by the project. The role of the exchange-rate function in a linear or logarithmic weighted cost-of-capital expression depends on the specific circumstances under analysis.

Second, the use of the formulas will also depend on the size of the project relative to the capital stock of the economy. We have treated here a case of projects in an economic environment characterized by nontransferability of domestic into foreign currencies. These projects have been assumed to be large relative to the composition of national income, and thus the investment bundle determines the average cost of capital of the country in the long run, and an optimal currency mix applies to these projects. In the case of "small" projects we would also suggest looking to a situation of multiple project facets rather than one project in a world of multiple currencies. In particular, if no transfer of domestic currency is possible, we should calculate an internal rate of return of the project assuming that it is fully financed in pesos and another rate of return of the project assuming that it is fully financed in dollars. The policy maker should then pick that "project" with the largest rate of return.

Third, it is important to distinguish between the environment surrounding the government and the environments of projects. In analyzing this setting, we must be cognizant of the linkage between the central planning office, the central bank, and the projects. Many times a scarcity of dollars is a direct result of government policies or laws which do not allow transfers of domestic to foreign currency. Government policies, such as favoring very low income groups, constrain a project to a nontransferability environment. In analyzing the impacts of this assumption we must take into account the fact that some institutional limitations, if not all of them, are removable. However, risk may be one of the nonremovable constraints.

Finally, we have ignored a broader social benefit-cost analysis in this financial analysis of projects. The literature seems to take the standard view that the analysis of social benefits and costs is independent of the financial environment of those projects; one extreme notion of this is represented by ranking projects using the IRR criterion and obligating the budget (regardless of multiple currencies) until it is exhausted. In this view, there is complete independence between a unit of net social cost of a project and a unit of the budget. However, this is not true; the basic linkage between the financial process and potential social benefits is through the balance of payments: tradable goods, foreign exchange policies, and the like. In monetary terms, some outcomes of these financial policies might be reflected in the interest rate and, thus, the discount rate used in selecting projects. However, we are mainly concerned with short- and long-term comparative advantages generated by projects through changes in liquidity and repayment of foreign debt of a country. These interrelationships will affect the profitability of projects and must be introduced in our general investment method.

The Investment Plan's Demand for Foreign Borrowing

Using the optimal composition of the economy's capital stock X^* given by the model, we will now discuss the determination of the total demand for foreign borrowings to finance the investment plan. From the model we have a vector of investments and corresponding activity levels of the type r_1X_1, r_2X_2, . . . , r_nX_n; where X_i represents project i, and r_i represents the optimal proportion of project i in the economy's portfolio ($0 \leq r_i \leq 1$). For the two-source-of-funds model, call α_{ij} and α_{2i} the optimal proportions of currency 1 and 2 in project i. The total demand, given the capital cost of uncommitted funds of the project, is determined by

$$\begin{bmatrix} \alpha_{11} \\ \alpha_{21} \end{bmatrix} r_1 k_1, \quad \begin{bmatrix} \alpha_{12} \\ \alpha_{22} \end{bmatrix} r_2 k_2, \quad \ldots, \quad \begin{bmatrix} \alpha_{1n} \\ \alpha_{2n} \end{bmatrix} r_n k_n$$

For example, if the capital cost of project i is 1,000 units (for a $\rho = 1$), $r = .50$ and $\alpha_{1i} = .25$, the total demand for dollars would be: $1,000 \times .50 \times .75 = \$375$, with the balance in pesos (125).

After calculating these amounts for each project, we can add all the required dollars and pesos to determine the total financial demand for pesos and dollars to implement the investment plan; call these units λ_1 and λ_2 respectively. In the case of n sources of funds, we will have a vector of n components: $[\lambda_1, \lambda_2, \ldots, \lambda_n]$.

Policy Implications

Foreign economic assistance plays a very important and rather complex role in developing economies; the need of borrowing to finance and accelerate economic development comes at the expense of a growing external debt. This issue is not new to the economic literature which has focused on two different perspectives: the macro- and microeconomics of foreign aid.

The macroeconomics of aid concerns the assessment of foreign assistance needs to sustain a given growth pattern. According to Mikesell (1964), there are economists who postulate that the required

amount of aid is directly related to the capital absorption capacity
of a country; the approach relies upon variations of the Harrod-Domar
models, and assumes a marginal saving ratio above the average ratio.
Others postulate that the amount of foreign aid must reflect the structural discrepancies of savings to investment (the domestic gap);
their approach focuses on import capacity as the major bottleneck
to investment and growth. Finally, some economists have developed
a theory to determine the demand for foreign exchange required to
satisfy the earning expenditures activities of a particular country;
they have conceptualized this need for foreign borrowings as it applies
to specific capital projects.

On the other hand, the microeconomics of aid is concerned with
the allocation of aid as functionally dependent on specific development
projects and programs. As for the macro approach, growth was the
principal objective. For the microeconomist the objective was the
maximization of economic efficiency defined in terms of potential
welfare improvements operationalized by using benefit-cost analysis.

The implementation of our methodology applied at this first level
of decision making will permit the total integration of the micro and
macro approaches to foreign aid. In this particular case, borrowing
and repayment capacity will be defined as functionally dependent on
a project's financial production function.

The absence of transferability of domestic currency into foreign
currencies for loan repayment will delineate and characterize the
optimal set of development policies.

> Mexico in its irrigation law establishes that the
> ejidatarios are exempted from paying any money to
> the government as a compensation for this concept
> [capital cost of the project]. In Venezuela the criteria
> followed has been that the initial investment will be
> recovered through the new taxes accrued to the govern-
> ment as a consequence of the increment of economic
> activity and the possibility to obtain taxes from peas-
> ants when they have substantially improved their
> income situation (Reina 1974, p. 33).

It is clear from this comparison how the law establishes the conditions for the transferability of currency.

In the Mexican case, the nontransferability assumption seems
quite justified. The mechanisms and institutional arrangements to
transfer pesos into dollars must be developed in other sectors to
improve the aggregate repayment capacity so as to finance agricultural projects and rural development expenditures. It does not
appear that the government cares about capturing the potential surplus

value of the project "gainers." This policy might result from an explicit recognition of the low level of income of the ejidatarios; their low level of savings makes it impracticable to rely upon the project's repayment capacity.

We see at least two important considerations here. First, relying upon other sectors' ability to repay foreign debt implies a further redistribution of income in favor of project beneficiaries which must be given explicit consideration in project analysis. This increased redistribution of income may have economic and social impacts which could worsen the general state of the economy.

Second, policies for self-sustained development, in addition to showing concern for the aggregate repayment capacity, should consider tariff and trade restrictions; protective intervention in domestic and foreign markets which might end up worsening the foreign trade position of the country and inducing unacceptable levels of trade diversion which could further worsen the balance of payments.

The reformulation of repayment capacity, under the extreme assumption of nontransferability, has specific implications for public finance policies. Under a situation characterized by an excessive foreign financing of certain segments of projects, the determination of the optimal mix (α) not only will decrease the social cost of investments but also will permit the financing of a larger number of projects.

The economics of project financing discussed in this section have specific implications for the formulation and implementation of agricultural and rural development projects such as land settlement and irrigation. Because of the structural characteristics of these sectors—low income per capita, underdeveloped market mechanisms, and the like—excessively foreign-exchange-financed projects may cause a significant burden to developing countries; opportunities to transfer domestic currency into foreign exchange to repay loans is limited. However, even during the "import substitution years" these projects might not have met the optimal mix criterion and yet the social cost might not have been excessive: many were probably Type I investments. We see the options as being relatively clear for these agricultural and rural development projects; the proportion financed in domestic currency must be very high, or the projects must be accompanied by specific recommendations and policy instruments to create the necessary repayment capacity.

The model presented here may also be used for more general purposes. As an illustration the α coefficient might be defined as an income-distribution indicator of those projects that have qualitatively distinguishable cash flows. For example, in those projects that benefit two identifiable classes of people (rich and poor) in which the benefits are rarely transferred from one group to another, α may

represent for the decision maker the optimal proportion of the total
costs of the project shared by both groups. The coefficient also
provides guidelines for finance policies concerning the extent to
which progressive and regressive taxes should be used to refinance
the project. The next section will cover some of the more salient
aspects of the second level of decision making: choosing among
different sources of funds.

FOREIGN-AID MANAGEMENT

The determination of an optimal currency mix and the total
amount of required foreign borrowings does not relieve planners
from choosing among different sources of funds. The source of
foreign borrowing has played a very important role in determining
the structure and character of developing countries' foreign debt,
and here foreign-aid management refers to the process of choosing
among different sources of borrowed funds. Recall from Chapter 5
that there are two ways of characterizing different sources of financing: functionally and statistically. The functional classification of
loans assumes that foreign assistance accomplishes certain functions
such as (1) long-term loans for financing specific investment programs; (2) long-term loans for general use, or balance-of-payments
purposes not attributed to specific projects; (3) loans by development
banks to developing countries; (4) loans which will perform the role
of monetary stabilization; (5) loans for financing specific exports
needed by the donor country; (6) loans for financing the production
of strategic commodities (weapons); and (7) loans with the purpose
of stimulating foreign private investment in regions of the world
characterized by insufficient economic growth (Mikesell 1964).

By way of contrast, the statistical classification characterizes
a loan by its attributes or potential impact on the recipient country.
Here, loans are classified by their interest rate, grace period,
maturity, and other attributes discussed in Chapter 5. This approach
of selecting a preference vector over potential sources of funds has
three major advantages which warrant mention. First, the possibility of incorporating a multidimensional set of attributes is a clear
and effective way of introducing a multiple-objective formulation
model. Second, the format will serve as a meaningful information
system for government planners and decision makers in light of a
multiobjective framework. Finally, as an information system, the
format will play a crucial role in the implementation and ex-post
allocation of different sources within the national plan of the economy.

As in Chapter 4, we will use goal programming to find the preference ranking over different sources of funds. As before, the objective

function is defined in terms of distance from prespecified targets, with a structural modification in the goal vector. In particular, we interpret the decision maker's directions of preference as increases in the value of an attribute; loans with high interest rates are "worse" than loans with lower interest rates, other things being equal. The modification of the goal vector is made with reference to the decision maker choosing the loans with the lowest interest rate, if this is the only attribute for selection. This implies a zero value for the interest rate in the goal vector. This procedure is repeated for all attributes under consideration.*

The empirical application considers the statistical attributes of 13 potential sources of funds, as presented by OECD (1974 and 1975). We consider a set of six statistical attributes: (1) interest rate, (2) maturity, (3) grace period, (4) grant element (subsidy element), (5) tied assistance, and (6) "composite index" ($g \times f$). The first four attributes for the years 1973 and 1974 were taken directly from OECD statistics. The sixth, the composite index, considered the importance of the total loans to the GNP of these countries ($g = \dfrac{\text{ODA loans}}{\text{GNP}}$) modified by the number of developing countries for which this country represents its principal donor (f). Both statistics are taken from ODA annual statistical yearbooks.

The source-of-funds matrix is presented in Table 6.2, and the vector of goals is presented across the bottom of the table. Both the number of years and attributes may be augmented for different situations. We have ranked the sources in Table 6.3 assuming equal preferences over the attributes, and assuming that preferences place a higher weight on the grant element of the loans.

In analyzing the results in Table 6.3, assume that the policy maker is trying to answer the question: "From which source should funds be obtained?" We have included in the source-of-funds matrix only foreign sources; the same exercise can be done using information for domestic sources of funds. If the policy maker does not

---

*The relationship between a loan's attributes and the goal vector is different from the one proposed for project selection. In this case we have to assess the policy maker's preferences and must assume that "more is better" or "less is better"; we then take distance to the origin or any predefined scale for example, percentage (0-100). Consider any nonpercentage element and take its inverse value, assigning a zero in the corresponding element in the goal vector if "more is better." For percentages put in the goal vector 100 or zero depending on the policy maker's preferences. Some of the values in Table 6.2 have already been transformed; for example, maturity and grace period.

TABLE 6.2

Source-of-Funds Matrix and Goal Vector

Statistical Attributes / Sources	Maturity '73	Maturity '74	Interest Rate '73	Interest Rate '74	Grace Period '73	Grace Period '74	Grant Element '73	Grant Element '74	Tied Assistance '73	Tied Assistance '74	Composite Index '73	Composite Index '74
Australia	.112	.125	3.00	3.00	.417	.250	30.5	30.1	19.2	26.8	.80	.90
Austria	.065	.750	3.90	4.00	.208	.286	36.7	31.1	19.2	19.2	.00	.00
Belgium	.036	.034	2.50	2.10	.116	.102	60.0	65.2	11.8	15.7	.00	.00
Canada	.020	.002	.10	.20	.101	.102	88.9	87.8	46.7	53.3	.60	.50
Denmark	.031	.032	.10	.10	.111	.111	81.4	82.0	25.2	25.0	.00	.00
France	.046	.047	3.40	3.40	.217	.217	44.7	44.7	19.9	19.9	14.4	14.2
Germany	.00	.030	2.10	1.80	.110	.101	63.6	68.6	22.8	9.2	6.0	8.1
Italy	.068	.050	4.30	4.00	.244	.232	32.8	38.3	10.9	2.9	.4	.8
Japan	.041	.043	3.70	3.50	.130	.139	46.6	47.5	60.6	54.8	1.7	2.2
Netherlands	.032	.032	2.50	2.40	.119	.123	61.1	62.2	33.5	25.3	.9	1.2
Sweden	.021	.024	.90	1.70	.100	.115	81.1	71.6	5.2	9.1	1.9	2.5
United Kingdom	.040	.041	1.10	2.00	.164	.149	66.6	67.7	24.5	24.5	10.7	13.5
United States	.025	.027	2.60	2.60	.093	.111	68.2	65.6	42.3	42.3	9.6	7.3
GOALS I	0		0		0		0		0		0	
GOALS II	0		0		0		100		0		14	

Source: Compiled by the authors.

120

TABLE 6.3

Ranking Sources of Funds

Source	Ranking I	Ranking II
Australia	12°	12°
Austria	11°	11°
Belgium	5°	6°
Canada	6°	3°
Denmark	2°	2°
France	7°	9°
Germany	3°	4°
Italy	10°	10°
Japan	13°	13°
Netherlands	8°	8°
Sweden	1°	1°
United Kingdom	4°	5°
United States	9°	7°

Source: Compiled by the authors.

reveal any preference for any particular objective we rank foreign sources in rank I (equal weights). This information tells the decision maker that, given the way the decision environment was characterized, the most favorable source of funds is from Sweden, then Denmark, Germany, and so on. If the policy maker wishes to utilize foreign funds that have the highest weight on net subsidy—the grant element—then rank II is relevant and Canada and Belgium offer, after Sweden, favorable sources of foreign aid.

The model can be used to discriminate among different capital flows for private enterprise, government, or any other decision unit. More sophisticated attributes of loans might be introduced such as the probability of negotiating an unpaid debt, the probability of getting the loans, and so on. We have used only OECD indicators.

FUND DISBURSEMENT, OR THE ECONOMICS
OF PROJECT IMPLEMENTATION

While it is difficult to treat such a complex and important subject in anything less than an entire book, we will give some basic outline to the major problems of disbursement of project funds and will discuss the implications for further analysis. It is to be assumed that the policy maker has identified the projects to include in the national plan and has determined the cost of these projects, their currency mixes, and the sources (domestic or foreign) from which funds will be obtained. The question now is how to implement the various components of the existing projects in an optimal manner.

In the traditional way of implementing and sequencing projects (or particular project activities), economists and engineers have generally employed techniques which give priority to the time element. Two traditional techniques which consider minimization of time as the principal objective are represented by the PERT (Progress Evaluation and Review Technique) model, and by the CPM (Critical Path Method) model. Both give the total minimum time and the ordering of critical activities to maximize construction efficiency of a project. With the use of computers, PERT has become a very useful implementation tool for technicians. However, in constructing or implementing projects we must carefully distinguish between those investments whose activities are orderable and those investments whose activities are not orderable. At one extreme there may be investments which, because of their technical processes, are not orderable; we cannot alter a technologically given sequence of events. However, there are other projects, such as rural development (multiactivity projects), which are basically orderable; we can sequence and build houses and roads, undertake land clearance, start personnel training, and the like, in a way which does not necessarily relate to the minimization of time or some other engineering criteria.

For purposes of the analysis we will assume orderable projects. Moreover, under circumstances characterized by orderable projects, we will show that there are many possible sequences, each of them representing "different projects." These orderings may respond to implementation of multiple objectives and/or to the institutional characteristics of the budget cycle. Finally, the analysis will draw attention to how construction periods may be used as an economic policy to change income distribution, employment, and, in general, development patterns.

Disbursement Criteria

The construction of a project in two years versus four years represents two economically different investments; just as there is an optimal time to begin a project, there is also an optimal length of time in which to construct the project. The multiple ways of constructing a project will be related to the existing multiple criteria for disbursing (expenditure) funds into this activity—one of the most significant acts of implementation. As stated before, one criterion might be to minimize the construction time, where time becomes the objective and expenditures the constraints. However, there are many other objectives which do not necessarily relate to minimizing time. Examples are maximizing employment, repayment of debt, and countercyclical economic policies. In particular, consider a policy maker who is trying to use a given project, to order project activities, to maximize the number of jobs created. Disbursement based on maximization of employment does not necessarily imply a critical path (minimization of time). Indeed, it could imply the possible extension of the construction period. This can be extremely relevant for many developing countries.

Consider, for example, Figure 6.3A in which we have money expenditure and labor on the vertical axis and time on the horizontal axis. An orderable situation may be characterized by the minimization of time; it is represented by curve A. The optimum time for construction is graphically represented by t_0. However, if policy makers want to order a project's activities in such a way that we maximize employment, the construction period—and the project in general—may be totally different, for example, t_1; activities might be ordered in such a way that we finance first that aspect with the largest employment absorption (see Figure 6.3B). These figures may be modified to introduce other objectives, such as income, foreign exchange, and the like. In all, these different alternatives for implementing a project (or a group of projects) give rise to different potential benefits to society. For the policy maker then, implementation of projects can become a problem of multiple objectives.

The expenditure-employment situation is complicated by the way in which disbursement of funds is constrained by the budget cycle. If the policy maker controls all the funds available for construction at $t = t_0$, there may be an expenditure pattern compatible with an optimal employment pattern. Nevertheless, under many circumstances this is not the case and it becomes difficult to find an adequate solution. The problem gets more complicated if more objectives are introduced; then, at the margin—and given the policy maker's

FIGURE 6.3

Different Lengths of Time for Constructing a Project

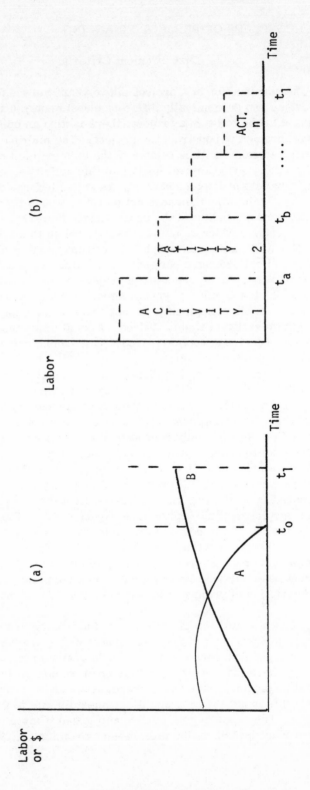

Source: Compiled by the authors.

124

preferences—per unit of money spent in the project there must exist
optimal conditions which reflect the ideal trade-offs among multiple
objectives.

Some Further Comments

Before closing this chapter we should stress the importance of
institutional arrangements in determining the budget cycle to finance
a group of projects and the limitations of presenting a reduced-form
formula of net present value of a project's worthiness. The first
problem relates to the former discussion on disbursement, taking
into account social costs of disbursement to groups of projects. The
second problem will point out the shortcomings of the NPV formula
and how economic analysis might be improved if we disaggregate it
to consider investments by stages (that is, at different points in time)
and by presenting its cash flow for different components. There are
specific social benefits associated with project financing and the
basic theory on discounted cash flows tells us that money tomorrow
is worth less than money today. This discussion will be particularly
relevant to clarify an old controversy: "money for projects or money
for programs." Assume, for example, that a project costs $100
and that the programmed disbursement schedule is 10, 10, 20, 30,
30. If the institutional setting, determining the ways and means of
the national budget, allows planners to have the $100 at their disposal,
the first year the economy will spend 10 and save not only 90 but the
interest rate earned on it, for example, 99, if the discount rate is
10 percent. If this money is distributed year by year on a project
basis, the economy is losing $9. Otherwise, when the project is
fully implemented the economy will have saved $31.26. The $31.26,
which we will call social benefits from financing (SBF) depends upon
two factors: the opportunity cost of capital and the disbursement
schedule. For an explanation of the latter, assume a disbursement
schedule 40, 30, 20, 5, 5 in which SBF is only $13.30 when the
discount rate is 10 percent.

To generalize we may assume that the policy maker, who
supposedly would always be investing what is frozen in the best
economic alternative, has a budget B, and a disbursement schedule
of d_1, d_2, d_3, . . . , d_n at a discount rate r. The SBF for any
particular year may be formulated as SBF = $(B_n - d_n) (1 + r)$ where
$B_n = (B_{n-1} - d_{n-1}) (1 + r)$.

The budget allocation in the way described above has immediate
indirect benefits when we introduce a new project; in particular the
policy maker could finance additional projects. Assume that another
project has a disbursement schedule of 10, 10, 10, 10; also, that it

FIGURE 6.4

Time Paths of Project Attributes

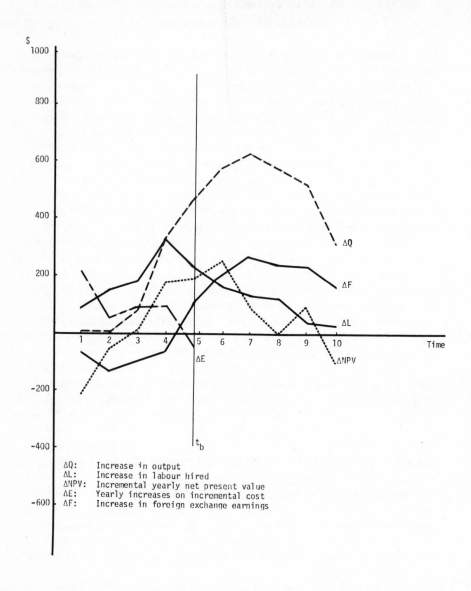

ΔQ:	Increase in output
ΔL:	Increase in labour hired
ΔNPV:	Incremental yearly net present value
ΔE:	Yearly increases on incremental cost
ΔF:	Increase in foreign exchange earnings

Source: Compiled by the authors.

is reproducing at a rate of 25 percent in a completely segmented
market with respect to the other. With the same $100 for the first
project we could finance the second one and have, in the fifth year,
a SBF equal to $20.

If planners do not have the opportunity of dealing with sophisticated models in considering multiple objectives, from a financial
perspective they might still disaggregate the NPV formula before a
project is approved. The reason for doing so refers to the fact that,
even though an aggregate NPV stream may seem to bring positive
benefits to the economy, it may not fulfill the objectives of the policy
maker in the relevant time horizon. Consider Figure 6.4: Assume
the policy maker is interested in increments to NPV, output, employment, foreign exchange, and expenditures. Also assume a time
horizon of five years (t_b). If there is a high weight placed on employment creation the objectives could be fulfilled even though $\triangle$NPV is
negative in the early stages of the project. Also assume that the
early output would be sold in domestic markets, but that in later
years the output could become a good source of foreign exchange.
A disaggregated analysis can be most helpful in gaining a better
understanding of project impacts; it is also the basis for the methodology proposed in our evaluation methodology.

SUMMARY

With debt-service obligations in the developing countries at a
very high level, and with new price levels for many commodities
traded in world markets—particularly petroleum—the economics of
project financing takes on new importance. This chapter has emphasized the problems in foreign-aid management which arise from
situations in which there are imperfect mechanisms for transferring
between domestic and foreign currencies. That is, when an investment project is primarily a producer of domestic currency, yet the
loan for that project must be repaid in foreign exchange, a developing
country may find itself in difficult times if other sources of foreign-
exchange earnings—say sugar exports—become uncertain or restricted.

Under limited currency-transfer assumptions, project evaluation
must include attention to the optimal currency mix for each project,
the optimal currency mix for the bundle of investments, the most
appropriate sources of foreign loan funds, and the optimal allocation
over time of these (and domestic) funds to the implementation of
projects. In this chapter we have given some suggestions for dealing
with these issues. We now turn to an illustration of the application
of the goal programming model to investment selection problems.

REFERENCES

Buchanan, Norman S. 1945. International Investment and Domestic
Welfare. New York: Henry Holt.

Chenery, H. B. 1953. "The Application of Investment Criteria."
Quarterly Journal of Economics, February, pp. 76-96.

Kahn, Alfred E. 1951. "Investment Criteria in Development Programs." Quarterly Journal of Economics, February, pp. 38-61.

Lombardini, Siro. 1969. "Quantitative Analysis in the Determination
of the Efficiency of Investment in Underdeveloped Areas." International Economic Papers, no. 9.

Mikesell, Raymond F. 1964. Mecanismos de Ayuda Economica
Externa. Mexico City: Estudios CEMLA.

OECD. 1974 and 1975. Development Cooperation: Annual Statistical
Yearly Bulletin. Paris: Organization for Economic Cooperation
and Development.

Polak, J. J. 1950. "Balance of Payment Problems of Countries
Reconstructing with the Help of Foreign Loans." In Readings
in The Theory of International Trade, ed. H. Ellis and L. Metz-
ler. Homewood, Ill.: Richard Irwin.

Reina, R. 1974. "The Problem of Development of Irrigation Areas
in Venezuela," Master Seminar Paper, May.

7

PROGRAM FORMULATION:
AN EXAMPLE

This chapter will focus attention on two decision-making questions that seem to be of particular value for policy makers. The first part concerns the general questions of project selection using a GP model, that is, optimal investment strategies under different assumptions of preferences, goal vectors, and budget availability, and the determination of the level of goal accomplishment of different strategies. The second part concerns a "constrained formulation" process that exists when one or more projects have been included, usually for political reasons, into the "optimal" investment strategy. As explained in Chapter 2, this second situation occurs at various stages during the investment formulation process.

We will present the methodology for the second level of decision making (Figure 7.1) assuming that projects are presented with a specific present value of net benefits (see Table 7.1, Investment Opportunity Matrix). Also, we will assume the CPO has provided the set of goals, or macroeconomic targets, whereby projects will be selected; these are presented in Table 7.1 Goal Vector. As mentioned before, these targets are usually provided by an input-output model, a regional development model, or a national account model. Every fiscal year the CPO presents to the ministry of finance the basic targets to be accomplished by the government investment program. For a planning period of five years, three sets of targets have been considered: regional income, employment, and foreign exchange. In this case they are presented as required increments in each year.

The next step considers the characterization and aggregation of projects based on the prespecified targets. This informational array is the investment-opportunity matrix; the components of this matrix were conceptualized in Chapter 5.

FIGURE 7.1

Policy-maker Level of Decision Making: First Level of Decision Making Assumed Constant

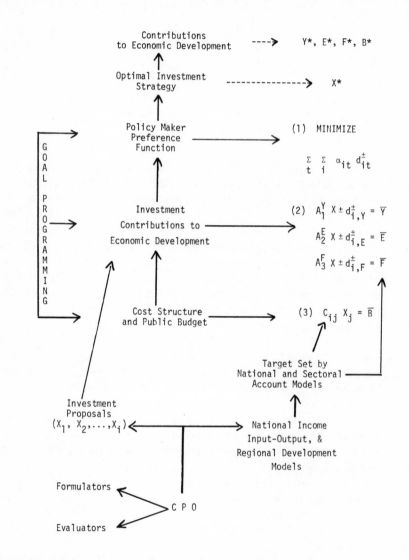

Source: Compiled by the authors.

TABLE 7.1

Information Needs for Investment Formulation: Investment-Opportunity Matrix and Goal Vector

(a)

Projects	Regional Income					Employment					Foreign Exchange					Net Present Value
$t=1$	1	2	3	4	5	1	2	3	4	5	1	2	3	4	5	
x_1	200	300	500	500	500	400	400	400	400	400	163	163	163	163	163	5000
x_2	200	300	600	600	600	400	500	500	500	500	150	150	150	150	150	4000
x_3	100	700	700	700	700	100	3000	3000	3000	3000	258	258	258	258	258	1500
x_4	100	700	700	880	880	100	3000	3000	3000	3000	250	250	250	250	250	50
x_5	300	400	400	400	400	200	800	800	800	800	150	150	150	150	150	1000
x_6	300	200	500	500	500	400	400	400	400	400	83	83	83	83	83	500
x_7	300	900	900	900	900	500	1500	1500	1500	1500	355	355	355	355	355	4000
x_8	500	1000	1000	1000	1000	700	2000	2000	2000	2000	410	410	410	410	410	3500
x_9	200	1100	1100	1100	1100	300	1800	1800	1800	1800	335	335	335	335	335	200

(b)

GOALS	Regional Income					Employment					Foreign Exchange				
G_1	2200	5800	6400	6400	6400	3500	12400	12400	12400	12400	2114	2114	2114	2114	2114
G_{12}	1100	2900	3200	3200	3200	1760	6200	6200	6200	6200	1057	1057	1057	1057	1057
G_{13}	2200	5800	2200	5800	3000	3500	12400	3500	12400	3500	2114	1000	2114	1000	2114

Source: Compiled by the authors.

131

While these tables characterize the physical aspects of each investment, they do not consider some financial and technological aspects of this process. Though we analyzed in detail the financial aspects of project selection (see Chapter 6) we have specified inter- and intrabudget constraints in the model. Finally, technological constraints refer to the nature of the selection process, such as assuming that projects are perfectly divisible or indivisible.

To summarize, this chapter will focus on the second level of decision making; it will show how the composition of the optimal investment strategy (stock) and the contributions to economic development (flows) are affected by changes in the policy maker's preference function, by budget availability, and by the various target levels. The second part of this chapter will assess the major stock-flow impacts of the imposition of politically selected projects.

PROJECT FORMULATION

Nine investment projects and three national objectives—regional income, employment, and foreign exchange—are considered. The planning horizon is of five years, in which an undistinguishable budget is spent on the selected projects during the first year. The length of the planning period is based upon the average number of years considered in many plans in developing nations (United Nations 1969 and 1970). Allowance for continuity from one period to another is provided. One way the decision-making model provides this continuity is by including those projects already under way ("old") with the "new" projects in the investment-opportunity matrix. If acceptance or rejection of one or more "old" projects is made through the political process, the constrained formulation model allows for these changes in the overall investment environment. If a complete new structure of a specific project is demanded by the government, it is possible to incorporate this into the reformulation model presented in Chapter 8. The following types of outputs will be analyzed in this chapter: (1) project selection; (2) macroeconomic impacts of alternative investment strategies; and (3) outcomes of sensitivity analysis to certain variables in the model.

Investment Selection and Multiple Objectives

Chapters 2 and 3 discussed some of the limitations of capital budgeting theory in the context of one objective optimization, and hence we will not go into the Lorie-Savage and Weingartner solutions to our numerical example. However, before presenting the basic solution of the problem it is important to review the informational arrays—the investment-opportunity matrix, the source-of-funds matrix, the available budget, the goals, and the weights on the various objectives—to obtain a perspective on the importance of this informational framework for policy makers independent of the model used.

In Tables 7.1, 7.2, and 7.3 we present some of the data representing the decision environment: IOM, goal vectors, cost structure of projects assuming an undistinguishable budget (SOFM), and the vectors of weights. Consider first the IOM (see Table 7.1). This is basic to any multiobjective decision and should present all projects' characteristics during the duration of the planning period (five years); this matrix must be revised periodically in light of changes which may affect the degree of goal accomplishment of any given project. Based upon this information, a "nonmodel"-oriented decision maker has several courses of action.

One course of action might be to accept the scores given by the NPV criterion and finance those projects whose NPV is greater than zero. The policy maker will know that this course of action is not feasible because the implied budgetary outlays likely exceed the available budget (SOFM 1, see Table 7.2). If these projects are comparable (see Chapter 3), they could be ranked by their contributions to efficiency, and then finance X_1, X_2, X_7, X_8 and, if it is perfectly divisible, a fraction of X_3. Again, if the budget is constraining, a subset of these might be chosen. However, if the policy maker wants to introduce new objectives (see Table 7.3) this solution may become suboptimal. For example, consider a situation in which a policy maker must decide on investments which contribute the maximum to employment. In this case a project such as X_4, rejected by the NPV criterion, might be fully financed.

The policy maker may select two objectives and reveal lexicographic preferences: choosing first those projects which maximize employment until a certain level is reached, and then choosing those which significantly contribute to, say, regional income until a given level of goal accomplishment is achieved.

Other situations may lead the policy maker to pick those projects which produce a maximum of any particular objective, or those which contribute the least to a certain objective, say environmental damage. The approach discussed here merely makes more explicit those choices always made by governments in developing countries; with the help of the model we can improve the efficiency of finding the appropriate solutions. This is particularly important when we introduce more than one objective, several investment projects, and a budget cycle of several years.

TABLE 7.2

Information Needs for Investment Formulation:
Source-of-Funds Matrixes

	(c) SOFM 1	BUDGET	(d) SOFM 2 Cost Structure of Projects for All Planning Periods				
	Costs and Budget in One Period		1	2	3	4	5
X_1	600		600	150	400	300	500
X_2	900		900	50	150	310	450
X_3	1300		1300	800	800	750	600
X_4	1300		1300	750	700	650	600
X_5	900		900	600	300	1000	50
X_6	900		900	400	800	453	450
X_7	1500		1500	750	600	550	350
X_8	1800		1800	25	200	300	450
X_9	1500		1500	1200	1000	800	600
$B_1 = 6000$		B_1	6000	4000	4000	3500	3500
$B_2 = 4000$		B_2	6000	4000	6000	2500	4000
$B_3 = 8000$		B_3	4000	6000	2500	6000	2500
		B_4	3000	2000	2000	1750	1750

Source: Compiled by the authors.

Given the data presented in Tables 7.1, 7.2, and 7.3 we will apply the GP model to illustrate first what happens when we have a one-year budget cycle. Second, we extend the analysis to a budget cycle of five years. Finally, we illustrate sensitivity analysis of changes in weights for various objectives, the goal vector, and the elimination of any project. To conduct this analysis it is necessary to distinguish two rather different situations: when projects are

TABLE 7.3

Information Needs for Investment Formulation:
Weights for Sensitivity Analysis

	Set of Weights Used for Sensitivity Analysis					
	$+W_1-$	$+W_2-$	$+W_3-$	$+W_4-$	$+W_5-$	$+W_6-$
Regional Income	1 1	5 5	1 1	1 1	1 1	5 5
Employment	1 1	1 1	5 5	1 1	1 1	1 1
Foreign-Exchange	1 1	1 1	1 1	5 5	1 1	1 1
Net Present Value					5 5	5 5

Source: Compiled by the authors.

perfectly divisible, and when they are indivisible and fractional projects give way to a discrete decision variable of "go-no go."

Perfect Project Divisibility

One-Year Budget Cycle. Under a set of parameters characterized by the values presented in Tables 7.1, 7.2, and 7.3, the GP model was applied and its results are presented in Table 7.4. Under the initial parameters (W_1, B_1, G_1), investment activities X_1, X_2, X_5, and X_6 would be rejected from the optimal bundle for economic development, while activities X_3, X_4, X_8, and X_9 would be fully accepted 100 percent financed with the available budget, and activity X_7 would be financed .07 percent. Thus the government would implement five projects during the five-year planning period, among which one of them will be only partially financed.

Sensitivity analysis can be conducted to better understand the formulation model. In particular, different sets of weights (W_2, W_3, and W_4 from Table 7.3), different government budget levels (B_2 and B_3 from Table 7.2), and different sets of goals (G_2 from Table 7.1) were introduced. The impacts on the optimal investment bundle are presented in Table 7.4 columns II-VII.

The sensitivity analysis makes possible the determination that project X_1 will be completely financed, as part of the optimal investment bundle, if high priority is given to regional income or foreign exchange savings, or if a net increase in the government budget is expected during this first year. Second, we can see that activity X_2 ranks very poor in terms of goal accomplishment. One of its features is that it is relatively cheap, which might lead the government to accept it fully if the goals are diminished: column VII of Table 7.4. Third, activities X_3 and X_4 are relatively productive in terms of goal accomplishment. However, they are relatively expensive, which would lead the government to reject them if the set of goals is cut in half: column VII of Table 7.4. Fourth, activities X_5 and X_6, under all different sets of assumptions, are never part of the optimal solution. Fifth, the acceptance or rejection of investment activity X_7 is very sensitive to the set of weights under consideration, in particular to the priority assigned to regional income. Moreover, this activity would be fully financed when a significant budget increase (B_3) or goal decrease (G_2) is introduced. Sixth, activity X_8's acceptance or rejection as a part of the optimal investment bundle is also very sensitive to the change in the set of weights. If regional income becomes the highest priority objective, this activity would be rejected; but if foreign exchange is of highest priority, this project will be partially financed (72 percent). Because of its high cost, the acceptance or rejection of project X_8 is very dependent on the budget level.

TABLE 7.4

Optimal Investment Strategy under the
Assumption of Perfect Divisibility and
Undistinguishable Budget in t = 0

Columns	I	II	III	IV	V	VI	VII
Assumptions	W_1 G_1 B_1	W_2 G_1 B_1	W_3 G_1 B_1	W_4 G_1 B_1	W_1 G_1 B_2	W_1 G_1 B_3	W_1 G_2 B_1
Projects							
X_1	0	1	0	1	0	1	.03
X_2	0	0	0	0	0	0	1
X_3	1	1	1	1	1	1	.57
X_4	1	1	1	1	1	1	0
X_5	0	0	0	0	0	0	0
X_6	0	0	0	0	0	0	0
X_7	.07	.87	.07	0	0	1	1
X_8	1	0	1	.72	0	1	1
X_9	1	1	1	1	.93	1	.26

Source: Compiled by the authors.

Finally, investment activity X_9 will always be accepted unless budget cuts are expected during this five-year planning period, or if a lower level of goals is assumed, in which case low-cost projects become dominant in the solution.

Budget Expenditures in the Planning Period. In this section a new change is introduced: The money cost of the projects is distributed in different years with the particular specification of the government budget for those years. The cost schedules are presented in Table 7.2. In the model we have assumed the existence of intra- and inter-budget transfers: what is saved in one period may be transferred to another.

The specific columns in Table 7.5 identify the type of assumptions introduced. The basic conclusion is that the optimal investment bundle is very sensitive to the type of budget cycle assumed. The optimal percentage of financing each of the projects may be read from Table 7.5.

Two basic changes are introduced for sensitivity analysis: elimination of a project from the opportunity set, and introduction of a new objective, net present value, which will be assumed to be of high priority.

Project X_4 was arbitrarily eliminated from the feasible set, and the exclusion transformed the optimal investment bundle into one where activities X_3, X_8, and X_9 should be financed fully, while project X_7 should be financed only partially (92 percent). All other investment activities would be rejected. This output is presented in Table 7.5, column VI. A continuous process of incorporation or elimination of a particular subset of projects can serve as a basis for analytically determining the extent of competitiveness, complementarity, and substitutability among projects.

The introduction of NPV radically changes the composition of the optimal investment bundle for economic development; the specification of new objectives in an economy implies developing a new set of optimal investment formulation processes which will become compatible with society's altered objectives. The result of this change is presented in column VII of Table 7.5. Given these assumptions, investment activities X_1, X_3, X_4, and X_7 will be those fully financed; projects X_2 and X_8 should only be financed 85 percent and 30 percent, respectively; all other investment activities should be rejected.

Perfect Project Indivisibility*

Here we will be concerned with decisions which involve the total acceptance or rejection of projects; no longer are projects subject to partial acceptance. One analytical approach is to transform the constraints in the decision set (X's) into a quadratic form by introducing three new constraints: $-X_j < 0$; $X_j - 1 < 0$; and $X_j(1 - X_j) \leq 0$. The most common solution is to apply an integer GP algorithm to avoid quadratic transformations. The basic solution of the problem is presented in Column VIII of Table 7.5. This transformation alters the optimal investment bundle substantially.

---

*See, for example, Wagner (1969).

TABLE 7.5

Optimal Investment Strategy under Different Assumptions Concerning Budget, Goals, and Weights

Columns	I	II	III	IV	V	VI (x₄ out)	VII (NPV)	VIII
Projects \ Assumptions	$\frac{W_1 G_1}{B_1}$	$\frac{X_2 G_1}{B_1}$	$\frac{W_1 G_1}{B_3}$	$\frac{W_1 G_1}{B_4}$	$\frac{W_1 G_3}{B_1}$	$\frac{W_1 G_1}{B_1}$	$\frac{W_5 G_1}{B_1}$	Perfect Investment Indivisibility of Projects B_1, W_5, G_1, Acceptance = 15, Rejection = 0
x_1	0	1	0	0	1	0	1	1
x_2	0	0	0	0	0	0	.85	1
x_3	1	1	1	1	0	1	1	1
x_4	1	1	1	1	0	–	1	1
x_5	0	0	0	0	1	0	0	0
x_6	0	0	0	0	0	0	0	0
x_7	.07	.87	0	0	1	.93	1	0
x_8	1	0	0	0	1	1	.30	1
x_9	1	1	.93	.27	.80	1	0	0

Source: Compiled by the authors.

139

Ranking of Projects

In the literature on benefit-cost analysis, a ranking is often made by listing the projects in order of their internal rate of return; those with the highest IRR have the first priority. Once a priority list is formulated based on the IRR criterion, implementation of projects proceeds down to encompass all those until we exhaust the last unit of the development budget. However, in a situation of multiobjective decision making and capital rationing, the IRR criterion becomes ineffective. Trade-offs among multiple objectives must be explicitly taken into consideration. For this purpose a transformation is made in the goal programming model, changing the $0 \leq X_j \leq 1$, or $X_j = 1$, or $X_j = 0$ constraints to a new constraint: $\Sigma X_j = 1$. The basic purpose is to derive a final vector of preferences which would rank all investment projects under consideration.

Courtney et al. (1972) made use of this constraint in determining urban-suburban location preferences and an illustration of their approach follows. Seven options for housing preferences were given to three groups of students. The output is presented in Table 7.6. Notice in this table that the structure of preferences in the first group favors option X_3, while groups 2 and 3 favor options X_4 and X_6, respectively. These outputs were also used to determine the expected number of people to be located in each of the seven options, given the average number of people in each strata (see bottom part of Table 7.6).

This approach is applied to the example here and a solution favoring X_8 over all other options is shown in Table 7.7. Then, in order to rank the other projects each is introduced, one at a time, to determine their respective impacts on the optimal solution. That is, because the program is constructed to minimize the deviations from the target goals, the selection of, say, project X_1 will increase the value of the objective function from its value at the optimum solution (only X_8).

How far the economy is from the optimum will depend upon the level implied by activity X_1. This notion of moving away from the optimum might be expressed by $\dfrac{\delta D}{\delta X_j}$, where D represents the objective function. This partial derivative tells the decision maker how far the economy is from the optimum state if δX_j of activity X_1 is included in the solution (other things remaining equal). The same derivative may be calculated for each of the investment activities included in the plan.

The ranking of these investment activities will depend upon the magnitude of these partial derivatives; that is, how far the economy will be from the optimum in terms of the accomplishment of objectives

TABLE 7.6

Vector of Preferences for Urban Location

(a) Urban-Suburban Preferences*

	x_1	x_2	x_3	x_4	x_5	x_6	x_7
Freshmen-Sophomores (no cars)	0.15	0	0.72	0.13	0	0	0
Freshmen-Sophomores (cars)	0.055	0.116	0.27	0.52	0.04	0	0
Juniors-Seniors	0.003	0	0.21	0.243	0.044	0.499	0

(b) Average Demand for Housing*

	N_1	N_2	N_3	N_4	N_5	N_6	N_7
Freshmen-Sophomores (cars)	120	0	580	105	0	0	0
Freshmen-Sophomores (no cars)	36	76	177	340	26	0	0
Juniors-Seniors (cars)	1	0	84	97	18	200	0

Source: J. Courtney, T. D. Clastorin, and T. W. Rueffli, "A Goal Programming Approach to Urban-Suburban Location Preferences," Management Sciences 18: 264.

TABLE 7.7

Solution Vector Given $\Sigma X_j = 1$, and Ranking Public Investment
by the Reduced-Cost Method

Investment Projects	Solution for xj=1 (W5)	RC (W5)	Ranking (W5)	RC (W1)	Rank (W1)
x_1	0	13935	3°	11995	8°
x_2	0	16100	5°	11160	7°
x_3	0	15360	4°	320	2°
x_4	0	20850	8°	0	1°
x_5	0	32100	9°	10560	6°
x_6	0	18335	7°	12195	9°
x_7	0	2975	2°	4435	5°
x_8	1	0	1°	1360	3°
x_9	0	17575	6°	2835	4°

Source: Compiled by the authors.

if the other projects are implemented. This criterion will be called the reduced-cost method. The values of these partial derivatives are presented in Table 7.7.*

To assess sensitivity, two sets of weights are used, with the second column including an output which considers NPV as an objective with the highest priority. The first column assumes a set of weights which treat equally all of the other objectives.

Macroeconomic Impacts

One of the most important features of the goal programming model is the possibility for assessing the macroeconomic impacts of the formulation and selection process. In this section the analysis will be expanded by establishing a direct relationship between project formulation and the macroimpacts of these projects. This analysis relates to how government, through the selection of an investment bundle, achieves the goals established by the prevailing plan. Three basic macroeconomic indicators were used to reflect the main objectives of the economy: regional income, employment, and foreign exchange. In this section we want to (1) show the accomplishment of macroeconomic goals, that is, the public investment impacts over the income gap, unemployment gap, and balance-of-payments gap; and (2) describe graphically the time path of the macrovariables under consideration.

In Table 7.5 we presented the sensitivity of the goal programming model to different parameters (weights, budget, goals) in determining the optimal investment composition. These investment bundles generate income, employment, and foreign exchange in a way described in Table 7.8. The columns of this table are equivalent, in terms of the assumptions, to the ones in Table 7.4. All of the columns in Table 7.8 are graphically represented in Figures 7.2 and 7.3, where the Roman numerals identify the respective columns. The slope of each time path represents the propensities which are the basis for defining the multiplier effects associated with the selected bundle of investments. Compare, for example, the generation of income and employment of bundles I and II (Figures 7.2 and 7.3, respectively).

Finally, the goals are changed under the assumption that the economy may be affected, for example, by an increase in private investment of other sources of exogenous shock to the GP model.

---

*We should emphasize that it is not possible to assume cardinality and infer that "this project is twice as good as that one." The method is also limited to perfectly divisible projects.

TABLE 7.8

Macroeconomic Impacts of the Investment Strategies Developed in Table 7.5

Attributes	Column	I	II	III	IV	V	VI	VII
	Assumptions	W^1 G^1 B^1	W^2 G^2 B^1	W^3 G^1 B^1	W^4 G^1 B^1	W^1 G^1 B^2	W^1 G^1 B^3	W^1 G^2 B^1
Income	t=1	920	860	920	961	387	1400	1117
	t=2	3560	3580	3560	3522	2427	4700	2900
	t=3	3560	3580	3560	3521	2427	4700	3200
	t=4	3740	3960	3740	3903	2607	5080	3207
	t=5	3740	3960	3740	3903	2607	5080	3207
Employment	t=1	1233	1333	1233	1406	480	2100	1750
	t=2	9900	9500	9900	9644	7680	11700	6200
	t=3	9900	9500	9900	9644	7680	11700	6200
	t=4	9900	9500	9900	9644	7680	11700	6200
	t=5	9900	9500	9900	9644	7680	11700	6200
Foreign Exchange	t=1	1277	1314	1277	1302	821	1771	156
	t=2	1277	1314	1277	1302	821	1771	156
	t=3	1277	1314	1277	1302	821	1771	156
	t=4	1277	1314	1277	1302	821	1771	156
	t=5	1277	1314	1277	1302	821	1771	156

Source: Compiled by the authors.

FIGURE 7.2

Employment Levels under Different Assumptions
of Objective Weights and Budget

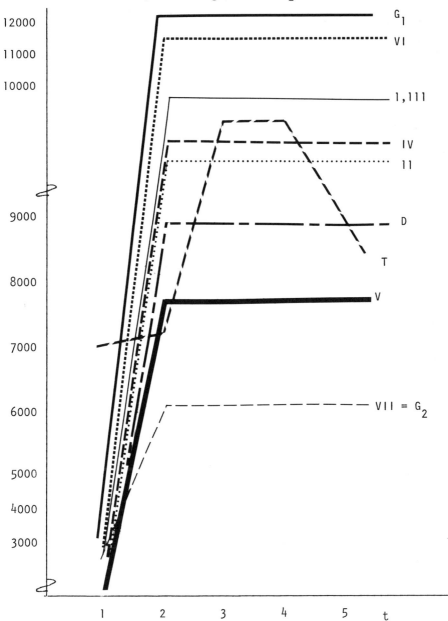

Source: Compiled by the authors.

FIGURE 7.3

Regional Income Levels under Different
Assumptions of Objective Weights and Budget

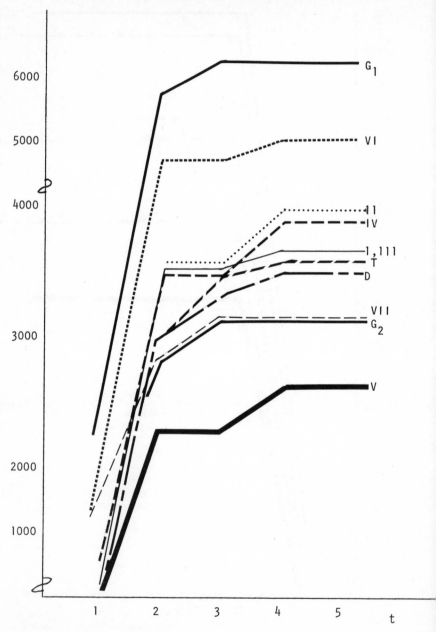

FIGURE 7.4

Foreign-Exchange Levels under Different
Assumptions of Weights and Budget

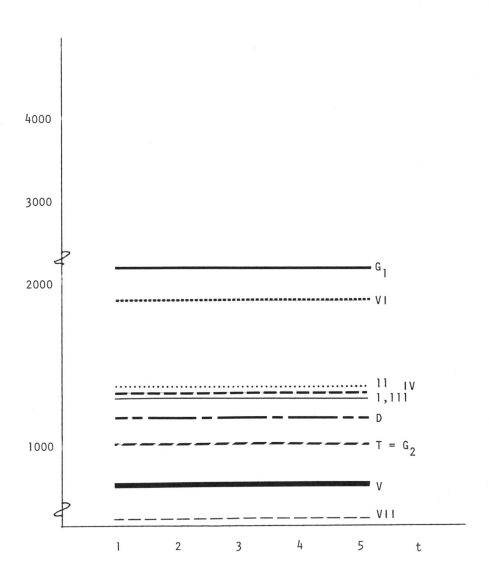

Source: Compiled by the author.

147

If these goals can be represented by G_2 (see Table 7.1), the time path and the multiplier effects of these macrovariables are presented in Figures 7.2, 7.3, and 7.4. The major conclusion here would be that, given the characteristics of the country's investment bundle, an income surplus and a full-employment economic state can be created at the expense of a large balance-of-payments deficit. The time path level, D, represents the macroeconomic impacts assuming perfect indivisibility of the investment activities (see Table 7.9). Project indivisibility implies a low achievement of goals, given the budget constraint associated with the projects.*

Sensitivity Analysis

To further explain the behavior of the formulation model, two major structural changes will be explored. One of them may repre-

TABLE 7.9

Macroeconomic Impacts of the Optimal Investment
Strategy When Total Acceptance or Rejection
of Projects Is Assumed

Period	Regional Income	Employment	Foreign Exchange
t=1	1100	1700	1231
t=2	3000	8900	1231
t=3	3300	8900	1231
t=4	3680	8900	1231
t=5	3680	8900	1231

Source: Compiled by the authors.

———

*Because the basic characteristic of the model is its easy integration with national account models through the goal vectors, the presentation of goal accomplishment has been done separately. Unification of the three targets might be accomplished by plotting on the vertical axis the percentage of goal accomplishment.

TABLE 7.10

Technical Coefficients of Employment Reflecting
Locational Impacts of Projects

Project	Period				
	t=1	t=2	t=3	t=4	t=5
X_1	1700	1700	1700	1700	1700
X_2	1500	1000	1000	1000	1000
X_3	50	70	700	700	700
X_4	100	100	800	800	800
X_5	1100	300	1800	1800	1800
X_6	3000	3000	3000	3000	3000
X_7	1000	2000	2000	2000	2000
X_8	50	150	180	180	180
X_9	25	150	200	200	200

Source: Compiled by the authors.

sent, for example, the locational impact of projects in the economy
(different regions of a country), changes in the structure of final
demand for inputs by each of the projects, or a situation in which a
different composition of the investment–opportunity matrix reflects
induced technical change.

This structural change is introduced by changing the a_{ij} coefficients associated with employment during the five–year planning
period. The new employment coefficients are listed in Table 7.10.
This structural change produced the expected change in the investment bundle composition and in the macroeconomic impact, which
is described in Table 7.11. These outputs may be compared with
those in column I of Table 7.5. The time path of the macrovariables
is presented in Figure 7.3 under the heading T. As can be seen,
during the first year there is a net employment surplus (that is,

TABLE 7.11

Optimal Investment Strategy and Macroeconomic
Impacts with Spatial Location Effects of Projects

| Project | | Macroeconomic Impacts | | |
	Period	Regional Income	Employment	Foreign-Exchange
$X_1=1$	t=1	1263	6944	1160
$X_2=.01$	t=2	2930	7535	1160
$X_3=.61$	t=3	3612	9735	1160
$X_4=1$	t=4	3612	9735	1160
$X_5=1$	t=5	2956	8735	1160
$X_6=1$				
$X_7=1$				
$X_8=0$				
$X_9=0$				

Source: Compiled by the authors.

large multiplier effect). The ability of the formulation methodology
to depict such changes is an important factor in decision making.

Now we will introduce "uncertainty" by illustrating the expected-
value solution introduced in Chapter 4. This will be accomplished
by making use of the data presented in Tables 7.1 and 7.10.

Each of the investment-opportunity matrixes represent outcomes
which have a known probability function. For example, the two IOMs
may be represented by A_{ij} and B_{ij}, where a_{ij} and b_{ij} are elements
of the matrix A_{ij} and B_{ij}, respectively. Moreover, assume that a_{ij},
representing the attribute j of the project i, will be achieved if the
project is located in region R, whose probability is p; and b_{ij} represents the attribute j of project i if it is located in region A, whose
probability is 1 - p. Under these circumstances, the expected IOM
of impacts will be represented by a C_{ij} array whose basic element

$c_{ij} = pa_{ij} + (1 - p)b_{ij}$. The Bernoulli Density Function is used here only as an example. Other types of functions might be used depending on the problem under consideration. The specific values are presented in Table 7.12.

If the generation of employment by a project in a particular planning year is 100 with a probability of .75 and 1,300 with a probability of .25, if located in a different region the expected value for the planner will be simply .75(100) + .25(1,300) = 400. This procedure may be used to represent expected technical changes, institutional changes, or any other structural impact to the economy.

Finally, sensitivity analysis can be employed using different sets of weights. In this analysis, high priority is given, simultaneously, to regional income and to net present value, assuming that the associated probability is .25. The output is presented in Table 7.13. The time path of these different stochastic alternatives is described in Figure 7.5.

TABLE 7.12

Expected Value of Generated Employment
with p = .25

Project	Period				
	t=1	t=2	t=3	t=4	t=5
X_1	1375	1375	1375	1375	1375
X_2	1275	875	875	875	875
X_3	63	1275	1275	1275	1275
X_4	100	825	1350	1350	1350
X_5	875	425	1550	1550	1550
X_6	2350	2350	2350	2350	2350
X_7	875	1875	1875	1875	1875
X_8	213	613	635	635	635
X_9	94	563	600	600	600

Source: Compiled by the authors.

TABLE 7.13

Optimal Investment Strategies under Different
Assumptions Relative to the Value of p
(probability) Using W_6 From Table 7.3

Project	p=1	p=0	p=.25	p=.25*
X_1	1	0	1	1
X_2	.85	0	0	.44
X_3	1	1	.63	0
X_4	1	1	.98	.85
X_5	0	0	1	0
X_6	0	0	1	1
X_7	1	.67	1	1
X_8	.30	1	0	0
X_9	1	1	0	1

*Using set of weights W_2 from Table 7.3

CONSTRAINED FORMULATION

The purpose of this section is to describe a situation which is
characterized by a process of project formulation in which certain
investment activities have been a priori (politically) selected. The
impacts on the process of formulation and selection of the public
investment plan will be the main concern of this analysis.

Because of political or other reasons, governments often decide
to implement projects even though they were rejected, or would have
been, at the formulation stage of the investment plan. The reason
may be the desire to protect a particular group in society, say the
peasants in a particular irrigation project. Additionally, there may
be an explicit desire to protect a bundle of inputs, the infant industry

FIGURE 7.5

Macroeconomic Impact of Projects for Different Values of p (probability of employment generation)

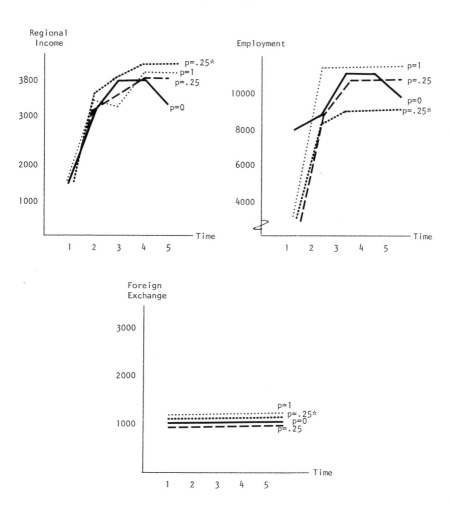

* p = .25* is computed from the set of weights given by W_2

p = .25 is computed from the set of weights given by W_2.
Source: Compiled by the authors.

argument; or the expected potentials of developing a particular sector of the economy with high political dividends. In general, this is frequently done, and the reasons are political in nature, or reflect a particular perception of the dynamics of the social system. The emphasis here is on the analysis of different impacts that these types of decisions involve, rather than on the merits of their existence.

Among the nine projects presented in Table 7.1, we will now assume that projects X_5 and X_9, which were initially rejected under assumed weights W_1, B_{11}, G_1, are introduced in the optimal investment strategy. This problem will be assessed assuming that all projects are perfectly divisible. Under circumstances characterized by a limited budget, other projects must now be rejected from the overall investment strategy. Moreover, if the composition of the capital stock changes, its macroeconomic flows will also change.

The program is here run for two sets of weights: W_1 and W_6 attributing to X_5 and X_9 a value equal to unity. As a result of imposing these two projects into the optimal investment bundle and maintaining the budget at B_{11}, projects X_2 and X_8 are totally rejected when preferences are as W_1. Also, project X_7, which was formerly fully financed, will now be financed only 27 percent. (Compare columns I and II of Table 7.14.) A change in preferences represented by W_6—regional income and NPV have a high priority—will change the optimal investment bundle again by rejecting project X_4 and introducing X_6 at a financing level of 73 percent.

Changes in the capital stock have produced significant changes on the macroeconomic impact on the economy. Comparing the unconstrained with the constrained formulation process (see bottom of columns I and II), we see that regional income will increase at the expense of employment, foreign exchange, and net present value. In the latter case (column III) where NPV is given as much weight as regional income, and compared with column II, we see that the economy improves its regional income in periods one and three; and its employment in year one; the others reflect a general deterioration (see Figure 7.6).

The model, then, will help planners to interpret political constraints—imposition of new projects—and preferences by critically presenting an informational framework such as the one presented in Table 7.14.

SUMMARY

This chapter, by using hypothetical data, has presented some of the features of the goal programming model for project selection. In a constrained or unconstrained formulation process, it has been

TABLE 7.14

Optimal Investment Strategy and Macroeconomic Impacts under Constrained Formulation
$(X_5 = X_9 = 1)$

		Optimal Investment Strategy		
		I	II	III
		W_1 B_{11} G_1	W_2 B_{11} G_1 $X_5=X_9=1$	W_6 B_{11} G_1 $X_5=X_9=1$
X_1		1	1	1
X_2		.85	0	1
X_3		1	1	1
X_4		1	1	0
X_5		0	1	1
X_6		0	0	.73
X_7		1	.27	.10
X_8		.30	0	0
X_9		0	1	1
		Macroeconomic Impacts		
Attribute		I	II	III
Regional Income	t=1	1818	980	1248
	t=2	3151	3440	3033
	t=3	3408	3440	3551
	t=4	3788	3820	3751
	t=5	3788	3820	3751
Employment	t=1	1648	833	1740
	t=2	8917	8400	6936
	t=3	8917	8400	6936
	t=4	8917	8400	6936
	t=5	8917	8400	6936
Foreign Exchange	t=1	1275	1251	1141
	t=2	1275	1251	1141
	t=3	1275	1251	1141
	t=4	1275	1251	1141
	t=5	1275	1251	1141
NPV		15,000	8817	15,000

Source: Compiled by the authors.

155

FIGURE 7.6

Macroeconomic Impacts of Alternative Investment Bundles: Assumption of Project Perfect Divisibility

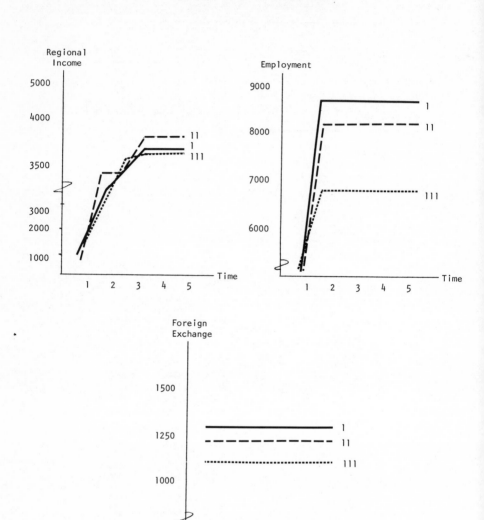

Source: Compiled by the authors.

illustrated how it is possible to illuminate the relationships among projects and their corresponding macroeconomic impacts. These relationships are highlighted by changes in preferences, budget, and/or economy's goals.

In the next chapter we will illustrate a decision environment where economic incentives applied at the project level play a fundamental role for the total economy.

REFERENCES

Courtney, J., T. D. Clastorin, and T. W. Rueffli. 1972. "A Goal Programming Approach to Urban-Suburban Location Preferences." Management Sciences 18: 258-67.

United Nations. 1969-71. "Titles and Time Periods of Recent Development Plans." Journal of Development Planning, nos. 1 and 3.

Wagner, Harvey M. 1969. Principles of Operation Research with Applications to Managerial Decisions. Englewood Cliffs, N.J.: Prentice-Hall.

CHAPTER

8

PUBLIC INVESTMENTS
AND BALANCED DEVELOPMENT
POLICIES: AN EXAMPLE

The previous example was concerned with a decision-making process in which accomplishment of a goal vector was a direct function of the budget, a vector of weights, and the optimal investment strategy of the economy. To accomplish those objectives the policy maker was characterized as choosing among investments within a given set of relatively unchangeable institutions. That is, the focus was upon a narrow view of the investment role of government. This chapter considers the other major role of government: as a rule maker. Here are explored a series of rule changes—institutional alternatives—given a fixed set of physical investments. General relationships among projects not only will reflect a limited budget but also will reflect interrelationships that depend upon the existing set of economic incentives.

This set of institutions to be analyzed here is represented by market and nonmarket incentives which affect the performance of individual projects, and hence the contribution of projects to economic development.* Given a fixed set of physical investments, there is a possible reformulation which will enhance the accomplishment of the macroeconomic targets in the economy. In this chapter we envision the policy maker as choosing among sets of institutions rather than among physical investments. There will be emphasis on the importance of a range of development policies upon the "worthiness" of investments and on their contributions to economic development. Policies related to incentives at the level of individual projects will in fact affect the performance of all projects. There might be policies which will change the allocation of resources of a given

---

*Most of the emphasis in this chapter will be on market incentives.

project, but there are others which will affect contributions of a number of projects to the economy. Moreover, there will be economic incentives which can affect the optimal investment portfolio but not the macroeconomic contributions, and conversely.*

The emphasis in this chapter will be on illustrating the usefulness of the decision model for fully appreciating the rule-making role of government. We will focus on alternative foreign exchange rates, on various proportions of exported output for a given project, and on the foreign price of project inputs and output. Throughout we will be using numbers from a hypothetical economy to illustrate the decision-making methodology.

A HIERARCHICAL MODEL

The approach to be taken here follows two earlier efforts. Levy and Sarnat (1975) developed a model to determine the general impacts of investment incentives upon resource allocation. This was analyzed by introducing three major investment incentives into a general net present value formula: income tax, rate of accelerated depreciation, and investment grants. The significance of these incentives, separately and together, is measured by induced changes in the internal rate of return and net present value of cash flows for given investment activities. Bassoco, Norton, and Silos (1974) developed a slightly different approach to determine how different policies affect the performance of irrigation projects and related investments. Three types of interdependence were analyzed: between projects and other policy instruments, among different kinds of investment projects, and between local and sector-level decisions.

While both approaches offer important insights into the development formulation and evaluation process, there are some limitations which are improved upon in this formulation. One major limitation of both efforts is the assumption that an optimal balance among different social objectives has been found. A second limitation relates to the substitution between projects; both consider projects as mutually exclusive rather than as alternative ways to achieve

---

*Recall the last part of Chapter 7; in that situation the political process imposed a given project—one which was relatively poor in terms of goal accomplishment—which planners could reformulate in such a way that it might contribute more to the economy. We can thus perceive of the policy maker as exercising rule-making power by applying incentives at the project level, or making use of certain rule-making alternatives to reformulate otherwise "poor" projects.

specific contributions to development in the context of multiple objectives. Third, no explicit recognition is given to the nature of project interdependencies; interdependencies which affect access to the flow of a particular resource, and which affect the way a resource generates different flows—such as income and employment—over time.

The major purpose of this chapter is to illustrate a methodology for determining the likely economic impacts arising from an array of economic incentives instituted at the project level;* the example will be an irrigation project which we assume has been selected as part of the optimal investment bundle. Initially we consider the relevant linkages between the hypothetical irrigation project and the various investment opportunities in a multiobjective framework. A hierarchical decision model will allow for consistent determination of the relationship between institutional changes and economic development. The hierarchical model is described by Haimes and Macko as one implementing coordination via "intervention inputs." These are parameters in the subsystems' objectives and constraints which are assigned by higher decision levels. Once this is done, the hierarchical model permits the restructuring of the model such that the overall problem is additively separable in the variables at lower levels in the hierarchy. Additionally, it is possible to form subsystem problems which can be solved independently of each other. Finally, a top-level optimum is attainable by coordinating the optimal solution of each of the subsystems in an iterative fashion (Haimes and Macko 1973, pp. 396-97).

The first level in this proposed model considers an irrigation project characterized by a linear programming framework which may be presented as follows:

Min: $C = \sum_i B_t(i)c_{jt}q_{jt}$ (Cost)   (8.1)

Subject to: $\sum l_{jt}q_{jt} \geq L_t$ (Land)   (8.2)

$\sum m_{jt}q_{jt} \geq M_t$ (Fertilizer)   (8.3)

$\sum k_{jt}q_{jt} \geq K_t(d)$ (Capital)   (8.4)

$\sum w_{jt}q_{jt} \geq W_t$ (Water)   (8.5)

$q_{jt} \geq 0$

———

*For simplicity we have taken only one project; the model may be easily generalized for n projects.

where c_{jt} represents cost per unit of output in each period; q_{jt} the output in each period; l_{jt} the land technical coefficients of production; m_{jt} the fertilizer technical coefficients of production; k_{jt} the capital technical coefficient of production; w_{jt} the water technical coefficients of production; L_t, M_t, and W_t the minimum requirements of productive inputs, K_t the minimum amount of required capital which is functionally dependent upon the rate of accelerated depreciation, d; and B_t the discount factor as a function of the interest rate.

It is assumed that the farmers on this project are cost minimizers in that they strive to minimize the expected value of costs subject to the constraints of the physical interrelationships of the irrigation system. At this decision level the model, for independent or simultaneous changes in the interest rate and rate of depreciation (i, d), determines the "optimal" production levels and resource allocation and, by its duality, the optimal shadow profit levels.* Once these output levels (q^*) are determined for different parametric values, the hierarchical model considers them intervening inputs into the linkage equations for the higher decision level. These equations consider income, employment, and foreign exchange in each of the periods, respectively, and are characterized by the following:

Employment Equation:

$$a_{1j}q_{1j} + a_{2j}q_{2j} + a_{3j}q_{3j} + a_{4j}q_{4j} = E_j \tag{8.6}$$

Income Equation:

$$[p_{q_{1j}}^d (1 - k_j) + \rho^Q k_j p_{q_{1j}}^W - \rho_j^F p_{F_j}^W f_{1j}]q_{1j} + [p_{q_{2j}}^d (1 - k_j) +$$
$$\rho^Q k_j p_{q_{2j}}^W - \rho_j^F p_{F_j}^W f_{2j}]q_{2j} + [p_{q_{3j}}^d (1 - k_j) + \rho^Q k_j p_{q_{3j}}^W -$$
$$\rho_j^F p_{F_j}^W f_{3j}]q_{3j} + [p_{q_{4j}}^d (1 - k_j) + \rho^Q k_j p_{q_{4j}}^W -$$
$$\rho_j^F p_{F_j}^W f_{4j}]q_{4j} = Y_j \tag{8.7}$$

Foreign-Exchange Equation:

$$[k_j p_{q_{1j}}^W - p_{F_j}^W f_{1j}]q_{1j} + [k_j p_{q_{2j}}^W - p_{F_j}^W f_{2j}]q_{2j} + [k_j p_{q_{3j}}^W -$$
$$p_{F_j}^W f_{3j}]q_{3j} + [k_j p_{q_{4j}}^W - p_{F_j}^W f_{4j}]q_{4j} = F_j \tag{8.8}$$

_____

*This particular problem of Min C = cq, subject to Aq > r, and q $\geq$ 0 has a corresponding dual problem that may be characterized

The labor coefficients (a_{lj}'s) are presented in Table 8.1 for each of the crops in a period of five years; $p^d_{q_{ij}}$ represents the domestic price of the output q_i in period j; $p^W_{q_{ij}}$ the world price of output i in year j; ρ^Q_j the foreign-exchange rate to the price of the outputs in period j; ρ^F_j the foreign-exchange rate price of the fertilizer in period j; k_j the proportion of output to be exported in period j; F_j the total foreign-exchange earning in period j; E_j the total employment generated in period j; Y_j the total income generated in period j; and f_{ij} the fertilizer coefficient.

The model determines the total values for E_j, Y_j, and F_j (E^*, Y^*, and F^*) as functionally depending upon input, output, and price coefficients, which then represent the new intervening inputs to the highest level of decision making by introducing these values into the investment-opportunity matrix. These E^*, Y^*, and F^* values are a function of government domestic and foreign policies. That is, they depend upon export proportion, domestic and foreign output prices, output and fertilizer exchange rates, and the foreign price of fertilizer as specified by the different equations' parameters.

The second level of the model will introduce the (E^*, Y^*, F^*) values into the IOM in the fashion already described above and will determine the optimal investment strategy and macroeconomic impacts in a multiobjective framework. This framework may be described by the following goal programming problem:

$$\text{Min:} \qquad D = \Sigma \alpha^{\mp}_{E_t} d^{\mp}_{E_t} + \alpha^{\mp}_{Y_t} d^{\mp}_{Y_t} + \alpha^{\mp}_{F_t} d^{\mp}_{F_t} \tag{8.9}$$

$$\text{Subject to:} \quad E^*X - Id^+_E + Id^-_E = \overline{E} \tag{8.10}$$

$$Y^*X - Id^+_Y + Id^-_Y = \overline{Y} \tag{8.11}$$

$$F^*X - Id^+_F + Id^-_F = \overline{F} \tag{8.12}$$

$$BX \leq \overline{B}$$

$$0 \leq X \leq 1, \text{ or } X = \{^0_1, \text{ or } X_i = 1 \tag{8.13}$$

---

by Max $\pi = ry$, subject to $A'r \leq c$, $r \geq 0$. By the duality theorem we know that at the optimum $cq^* = ry^*$, and $\partial \pi / \partial r = y_j \leq 0$, in which $y_j \leq 0$ for $r = 0$, and $y = 0$ for $r > 0$. In this case y represents a nonpositive shadow profit which reflects how much less of the full cost (c) the manager is willing to pay as a direct function of the resource utilization levels.

TABLE 8.1

Attributes of Project X5

Minimum Amount of Inputs Required

Input	Year 1	2	3	4	5
Land	5400	5400	5400	5400	5400
Capital	92	92	92	92	92
Fertilizer	97	123	173	111	73
Water	39.7	39.7	39.7	38.5	40.0

Cost Coefficients

Output	Year 1	2	3	4	5
q_1	16	22	36.3	20	24
q_2	11	14.3	20.6	22.6	12.4
q_3	14	14.3	16.9	20	44.3
q_4	13	14.3	21.2	18.6	21.3

Labor Coefficients

Output	Year 1	2	3	4	5
q_1	42	42	42	42	42
q_2	100	100	100	100	100
q_3	20	20	20	20	20
q_4	28	50	60	70	80

System of Equation's Initial Parameters

	Year 1	2	3	4	5
Domestic Price of Output (P_q^d)					
q_1	4	5	7	7	7
q_2	40	35	20	22	24
q_3	15	18	26	32	16
q_4	20	24	30	21	19
Foreign Price of Output (ρ_q^w)					
q_1	50	50	50	50	50
q_2	50	50	50	50	50
q_3	50	50	50	50	50
q_4	50	50	50	50	50
Foreign Price of Fertilizer (p_F^W)	.10	.10	.10	.10	.10
Exchange Rate Output (ρ_j^q)	1	1	1	1	1
Exchange Rate Fertilizer (p_j^F)	1	1	1	1	1
Proportion of Output Exported (k)	.75	.75	.75	.75	.75

(continued)

163

(Table 8.1 continued)

Irrigation Project X_5:   Input Coefficients

	Year	Output			
		q_1	q_2	q_3	q_4
Land	1	5000	1000	4000	2500
	2	5000	1000	4000	2500
	3	5000	1000	4000	2500
	4	5000	1000	4000	2500
	5	5000	1000	4000	2500
Capital	1	20	30	20	25
	2	20	25	25	27
	3	20	20	10	25
	4	20	20	20	20
	5	20	10	25	20
Fertilizer	1	101	40	10	15
	2	60	50	10	20
	3	35	80	10	15
	4	14	40	60	25
	5	14	20	10	25
Water	1	2	15	5	8
	2	2	15	5	8
	3	2	15	5	8
	4	2	15	5	8
	5	2	15	5	8

Source: Compiled by the authors.

where E^*, Y^*, and F^* represent the employment, income, and foreign-exchange contributions of all projects under consideration, and B represents a matrix of costs (the budget constraint).

To summarize the major sequential steps of the hierarchical model, the first level of decision making is concerned with the impacts of rule changes at the project level upon the allocation of resources. The levels of output (q^*) are introduced into the linkage equations to determine the project's contributions to economic development (E, Y, F). At the highest level the model determines—

considering the potential institutional arrangements that may exist
at the linkage level—the optimal investment bundle of the economy
and the macroeconomic impacts in a multiple objective framework.
A flow chart of the hierarchical model is presented in Figure 8.1.

This process of interactive development planning is carried out
by determining the relevant flows existing between the project and
the other projects of the economy's investment plan. The first step
considers the linkage between the policy instruments and the structure of the project (see upper left portion of Figure 8.1). The assumption here is that this linkage has a complex conformation composed
by two structural flows: one at the level of project technology, and
the other at the level of project generation of income, employment,
and foreign exchange. At the level of project technology, the interest
rate and the real rate of depreciation will be introduced, while at
the other level, export proportion, foreign-exchange rate, and foreign
prices, of inputs and outputs, will be the basic set of rulemaking
alternatives (see the upper middle portion of Figure 8.1). These
policies may be applied by fiat to the irrigation project, or by the
implementation of organizational and administrative arrangements,
such as marketing boards, direct price controls, credits, taxation,
or any other means of institutional arrangement.

The second step considers the modifications made at the first
step, introducing them into the IOM by assessing the new levels of
projects' contributions to economic development. This step will
determine the impacts—of the policies brought at the project level—
upon composition of the optimal investment strategy of the overall
economy. These impacts will be reflected through changes in the
macroeconomic levels of the economy's goals, and by the bundle of
projects that is finally selected. Given that the model is operating
under conditions of inelastic supply of capital, and that the economy
seeks to accomplish a set of preestablished goals, changes in the
IOM will modify the composition of the optimal investment strategy
and the macroeconomic impacts of all the projects.

This model allows two different administrative agencies—one
dealing with the specific project (that is, ministry of agriculture)
and the other dealing with the implementation of the economy's plan
(that is, central planning office)—to specify the basic criteria for
determining the optimal combination of spending and rule-making
roles of the government for accomplishing the highest level of
economic development.

The first step in operationalizing the decision-making model
requires the definition of the hypothetical project and the specification
of its assigned initial values which attempt to reflect the initial state
of production (see Table 8.1). Once this is accomplished, it is
possible to explore the role of alternative institutional structures—
this is the subject of the following section.

FIGURE 8.1

The Hierarchical Model

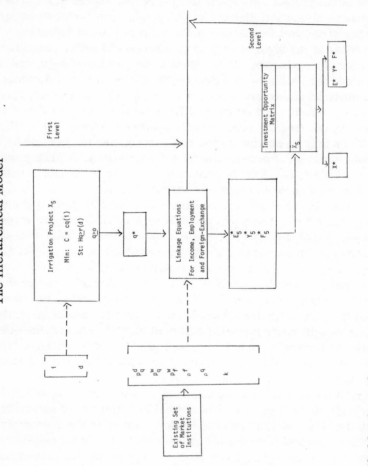

Source: Compiled by the authors.

GOVERNMENT AS A RULE MAKER:
AN EXAMPLE

This section will present, in a systematic form, the outlines of a "reformulation decision-making model"; the main purpose being to show that, assuming the set of physical investments is bounded, it is possible to analyze specific development flows by introducing a whole range of rule-making alternatives. The analysis will be concerned mainly with the changes different economic incentives produce over three significant elements that determine the developmental patterns in this model: (1) allocation of resources in the hypothetical irrigation project, (2) changes in the optimal investment strategy of the economy, and (3) real contributions to economic development. The allocation of resources will be analyzed, taking into consideration the changes produced by different economic incentives upon the level of use of a particular resource, the real willingness to pay (perfect competitive price minus the shadow profits) for the resource, and the output patterns generated. The changes in the optimal investment bundle and the macroeconomic impacts will be presented here by analyzing the optimal financing levels (acceptance or rejection) of the given projects and their contribution to the generation of income, employment, and foreign exchange.

Interest Rate and Depreciation Policies

Many levels of interest rate and depreciation allowances have been introduced into the model, and these different economic incentives have an impact, separately and together, upon the allocation of resources at the project level, and upon the optimal investment strategy of the economy.

As an example of how the model can illustrate these impacts, we present in Figures 8.2 and 8.3 an example of the combined impacts of different pairs of i and d upon the level of production and upon the shadow profit levels. Specifically, in Figure 8.2 we see that for different (i, d) products q_1 should be produced only in the first and last periods, and q_3 should not be produced during the first and the last period. For the other products and during different years, ideal production levels of particular commodities depend upon the combination of i and d imposed by government. In particular, we also see that it is possible to detect a certain complementarity between q_2 and q_3 with q_4; decreasing production of the former products increases the production of the latter.

Changes in economic incentives can also be reflected in the accounting prices of inputs. As presented in Figure 8.3, shadow

FIGURE 8.2

Production Implications of Different Combinations of Interest Rates and
Depreciation (i, d) for Project X_5
(four possible outputs $[q_{ij}]$ and five time periods $[q_j]$)

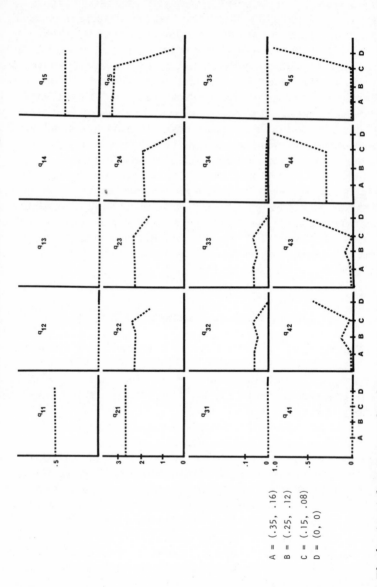

A = (.35, .16)
B = (.25, .12)
C = (.15, .08)
D = (0, 0)

Note: The horizontal axes consider four pairs: (.35, .16), (.25, .12), (.15, .03) and (0.0, 0.0). The vertical axes measure units of q_{ij}'s (output).

Source: Compiled by the authors.

FIGURE 8.3

Shadow-profit Implications of Different Combinations of Interest
Rates and Depreciation (i, d) for Project X_5
(four possible inputs and five time periods)

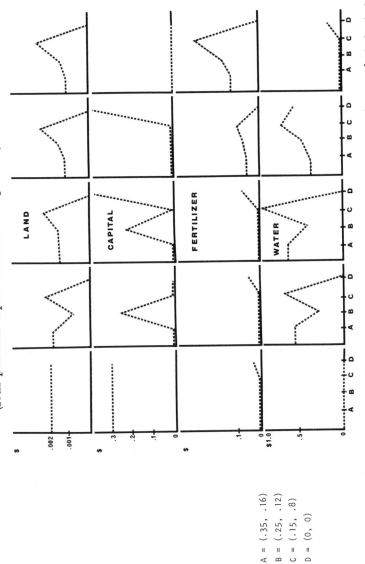

A = (.35, .16)
B = (.25, .12)
C = (.15, .8)
D = (0, 0)

Note: The horizontal axes consider four pairs: (.35, .16), (.25, .12), (.15, .08), and (0.0, 0.0).
Source: Compiled by the authors.

profits of inputs change drastically with changes in i and d. These changes will modify the optimal way in which resources should be allocated on a project. The study of these fluctuations in accounting prices will give the policy maker a framework for policies concerning pricing, taxes, and subsidies which could be very useful in correcting market distortions at the project level.

It is possible, using similar methods, to investigate the impacts of different government rules on various development goals such as income, employment, and foreign exchange. For this assessment we utilize a slightly different combination of interest rate and depreciation (A: i = 0, d= .07; B: i = 10, d = .07; and C: i = 20, d = .10) and use them in a sensitivity analysis concerning the acceptance of projects as well as macroeconomic effects. The results of this test are shown in Table 8.2 and in Figure 8.4. In terms of the investment bundle a move from (i, d) set A to either B or C causes project X_2 to be replaced by project X_8. The lower portion of Table 8.2 (and Figure 8.4) shows how the impacts upon goals can be assessed.

Policies in Export Markets

In this section we explore the first of five alternative variables—some of which are beyond the control of the government—as they relate to the optimal investment bundle and to the degree of goal achievement. The five variables are (1) proportion of output exported (d), (2) exchange rate for output, (3) exchange rate for inputs, (4) foreign price of inputs, and (5) foreign price of output. In the analysis of these economic factors we will assume that project X_5 has an interest rate of .15 and a rate of depreciation of .07. These five economic factors assessed for project X_5 will change the parameters in the set of income, employment, and foreign-exchange equations, which will then introduce changes at the formulation stage through the IOM. That is, Table 8.1 shows the initial parameters for the above five factors, as well as the initial requirements for project X_5. By incrementally introducing slight changes in one of the above five factors we can derive a new display of the optimal capital structure (the investment bundle), and the macroeconomic impacts; the former appears in the upper portion of Table 8.3, while the latter appears in the lower portion.

We present here, in a summarized form, the type of information possible from the exercise of adjusting policy variables within the context of the optimizing framework. These changes are modeled by introducing a series of values into equations 8.7 and 8.8, and the results are depicted in Table 8.3.

TABLE 8.2

Impact of Interest Rate and Depreciation Policies upon the Optimal Investment Bundle and Macroeconomic Contributions

	A (i=0.0) (d=.07)	B (i=.10) (d=.07)	C (i=.20) (d=.10)
Projects	Degree of Financing		
X_1	1.00	1.00	1.00
X_2	.44	.00	.00
X_3	1.00	1.00	1.00
X_4	1.00	1.00	1.00
X_5	1.00	1.00	1.00
X_6	.00	.00	.00
X_7	1.00	1.00	1.00
X_8	.00	.22	.22
X_9	.00	.00	.00
Macroeconomic Contributions			
Income			
t=1	835	857	857
t=2	2647	2736	2744
t=3	2765	2721	2753
t=4	2965	2921	2980
t=5	2988	2944	3000
Employment			
t=1	1550	1527	1527
t=2	8383	8605	8609
t=3	8396	8619	8656
t=4	8402	8625	8644
t=5	8425	8647	8730
Foreign-Exchange			
t=1	1199	1223	1223
t=2	1205	1229	1238
t=3	1199	1224	1251
t=4	1204	1228	1278
t=5	1209	1234	1284

Source: Compiled by the authors.

171

FIGURE 8.4

Macroeconomic Impacts of Various Interest
Rate and Depreciation Policies

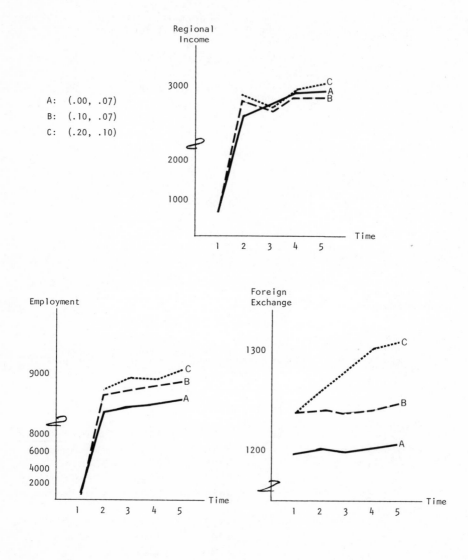

A: (.00, .07)
B: (.10, .07)
C: (.20, .10)

Source: Compiled by the authors.

TABLE 8.3

Significance of Rule-making Alternatives upon the Optimal Investment Strategy and Macroeconomic Contributions

Project	Proportion Exported			Exchange Rate (Output)			Exchange Rate (Inputs)		Foreign Price of Fertilizer			Foreign Price of Output			
	.30	.50	.75	1.7	5.0	25.0	0.0	1.50	0.05	0.10	2.00	1.0	10.0	45.0	60.0
	(1)	(2)	(3)	(4)	(5)	(6)	(7)	(8)	(9)	(10)	(11)	(12)	(13)	(14)	(15)
X_1	1.00	1.00	1.00	1.00	1.00	.91	1.00	1.00	1.00	1.00	.99	1.00	1.00	1.00	1.00
X_2	.00	.00	.44	.00	.00	.00	.44	1.00	.00	.00	.00	.00	.03	.00	.00
X_3	1.00	1.00	1.00	1.00	1.00	1.00	1.00	1.00	1.00	1.00	1.00	1.00	.90	1.00	1.00
X_4	1.00	1.00	1.00	1.00	1.00	1.00	1.00	1.00	1.00	1.00	1.00	.00	.00	.00	.71
imposed X_5	1.00	1.00	1.00	1.00	1.00	1.00	1.00	1.00	1.00	1.00	1.00	1.00	1.00	1.00	1.00
X_6	.00	.00	.00	.00	.00	.00	.00	.00	.00	.00	.00	.00	.00	.17	.86
X_7	.00	.27	1.00	.00	.00	1.00	1.00	.67	.95	.87	1.00	.93	1.00	.83	1.00
X_8	1.00	.00	.00	1.00	.22	.25	.00	.00	.26	.32	.22	1.00	1.00	1.00	.00
X_9	.07	1.00	.00	.07	1.00	.00	.00	.00	.00	.00	.00	.00	.00	.00	.00

(continued)

(Table 8.3 continued)

Macroeconomic Contributions															
Income															
t=1	886	579	490	874	1723	767	490	503	761	782	750	1119	750	1135	774
t=2	1255	1300	267	1404	1708	6287	381	770	6094*	6117*	5800*	5725	5800*	5800*	5800*
t=3	1359	1409	402	1417	1721	6400	476	723	6400*	6400*	201	441	761	458	680
t=4	1228	1271	231	1393	1667	6351	350	752	6111	6135	394	222	3438	421	597
t=5	1349	1399	391	1444	1760	6311	464	700	6348	6326	174	505	855	406	516
Employment															
t=1	1592	1305	1550	1592	1327	6806	1290	548	7015*	6922*	293	359	121	561	733
t=2	8781	8861	8583	8781	8905	8629	8383	8161	8613	8626	8238	2410	384	564	642
t=3	8794	8874	8396	8794	8919	8642	8396	8174	8626	8639	8619	7074	8619	3935	766
t=4	8800	8880	8402	8800	8925	8648	8402	8180	8632	8645	8625	7080	8625	6901	7636
t=5	8823	8903	8425	8823	8947	8671	8425	8203	8655	8668	8648	7103	8648	6924	7659
Foreign-Exchange															
t=1	1136	1166	1199	1209	1203	1237	1199	1164	425	1226	955	1250	1138	1269	1153
t=2	1143	1192	1205	1217	1229	1239	1205	1170	626	1231	1026	1275	1142	1276	1160
t=3	1137	1186	1199	1211	1224	1239	1199	1164	373	1227	938	1269	1137	1270	1154
t=4	1143	1191	1204	1216	1228	1237	1204	1169	648	1230	1045	1273	1143	1274	1158
t=5	1147	1197	1210	1222	1234	1239	1210	1175	876	1235	1114	1280	1147	1281	1165

* Over-accomplishment of goals

*Overaccomplishment of goals.

t — "Imposed" by government.

Source: Compiled by the authors.

174

The policy maker can be presented with this informational array which explains the main impact of changing market institutions. Let us assume, for example, that it is agreed to finance a bundle such as $X_1 = X_3 = X_4 = X_5 = X_8 = 1$, $X_9 = .07$, $X_2 = X_6 = X_7 = 0$. Then, consider two institutional options: (1) allow 30 percent of the products of project X_5 to be exported; or (2) give a more favorable foreign-exchange rate on exportable commodities, say 1.7 "pesos per dollar." A favorable exchange rate produces more foreign exchange and more income; although higher export quotas, in this example, generate more employment.

The same informational array can be used to assess a situation of rather equal contributions to any particular objective but arising from a quite different capital stock. Compare, as a matter of illustration, the case of an export quota of 30 percent (column 1) and a foreign price of output of 10 (column 10). In this case the table reveals an almost equal contribution to foreign exchange arising from a substantially different investment bundle. As a final comparison consider columns 3 and 7. Here we see that an almost identical capital stock can result in quite different income implications. Thus, the hierarchical model can be used to illustrate a variety of implications to the policy maker.

SUMMARY

The bulk of this book, and the majority of the literature on decision making in developing countries, focuses on the role of government as an investor in projects. Little attention is given to the important role of government as a rule maker. The purpose in this chapter has been to remind the reader of the important role of institutional changes at the project level and to illustrate the usefulness of the goal programming model for analysis of these rule changes.

This discussion was facilitated by postulating a situation in which a nonoptimal investment portfolio was undertaken. That is, we assumed that a project (X_5) was included in the investment bundle even though it would have been rejected by a strict application of the optimization model; we assume that its political merits—though not included as relevant considerations in the hierarchical model— were such that it was included anyway. Then, the analyst's job is to explore those institutional changes at the project level which will mitigate the bulk of the costs imposed by the inclusion of an inferior component into the investment bundle. We have explored institutional changes such as adjustments in the proportion of output from this project which is exported, changes in the foreign-exchange rate for the project's output, changes in the foreign-exchange rate for inputs used in the project, changes in the foreign price of these inputs, and changes in the foreign price of output.

Throughout, the purpose has been to illustrate the ways in which the analyst might employ the goal programming model to assess the likely impacts of these alternative institutional possibilities.

REFERENCES

Bassoco, L. M., R. D. Norton, and J. S. Silos. 1974. "Appraisal of Irrigation Projects and Related Policies and Investment." Water Resources Research 10, no. 6 (December): 1071-79.

Haimes, Y. Y., and D. Macko. 1973. "Hierarchical Structures in Water Resources System Management." IEEE Transactions, July: 396-402.

Levy, H., and M. Sarnat. 1975. "Investment Incentives and the Allocation of Resources." Economic Development and Cultural Change 23, no. 3 (April): 431-51.

CHAPTER

9

CONCLUSIONS

The essence of the development process in low-income countries is the selection of a configuration of investments and rules which enhances the possibilities of improved social well being at a certain cost. Part of these costs will be domestic resource costs, part will be foreign exchange costs, part will be other opportunities foregone, and part will be perverse incentives which must be incurred in order to move beyond the present situation. Of course, this list is not mutually exclusive, but a detailing tends to remind us of the exact nature of what is being given up and what is, hopefully, being gained. Another aspect of development, and one that sets it apart somewhat from economic activity in other more advanced economies, is the deterministic nature of the planning process; it is not the indicative planning of France, nor is it the virtual absence of planning of the United States. Here, we are dealing with the determination of production, employment, and foreign exchange targets which are then objectives toward which most of the economic activity is directed. Yet another aspect of development is the extent to which many of the economies are absent the rich natural resources base—and the extraction technology—of the more advanced economies. And, often what resources do exist have been under the control of the more advanced economies through ties that may go back to colonial times. Related to this is the degree to which these developing economies are constantly buffeted by decisions made elsewhere in the world with significant domestic impacts. To a country that earns 70-80 percent of its foreign exchange by exporting, say, sugar, changes in the world price of sugar or changes in import quotas by, say, the United States can have devastating impacts. Like the small, marginal firm of conventional microeconomics, the developing country constantly must struggle against a larger economic and political

environment which can largely influence its ability to survive.
Developing countries—just like small firms—face a decision-making
climate which is totally different from that in more developed countries. Coupled with this we have the cultural dimension which means
that methods and approaches which may work in a developed country
will not work at all in a developing country.

For some time now, economists writing about decision making
in developing countries have tended to focus on the evaluation of
investment alternatives at the project level. Benefit-cost analysis
has flourished under this interest in project-by-project evaluation
of investment possibilities. But, decision making in developing
countries is far broader than this attention on individual projects.
It is explicit recognition of the dual roles of government—as an
investor and as a rule maker. Decision making in developing countries is more than showing concern with the net present value of a
bundle of investment options and concern for the appropriate decision
criteria. Decision making is more than the search for reasonable
loans with which to finance a collection of projects. Decision making
is more than waiting for the ministries of transportation, agriculture,
water resources, and education to compile a "shelf" of projects with
positive benefit-cost estimates from which the ministry of finance
and the central planning office will choose enough to exhaust the
available budget.

Effective decision making in developing countries is first of all
recognizing the need to somehow bridge the gap between planners/
economists at the agency level and policy makers in the ministry of
finance, the central planning office, and the chief executive's office.
Second, it is a linking of project efficiency with efficiency in the
larger economic setting. That is, high present-valued net benefits
for certain investments may not result in the generation of many jobs
for the currently unemployed (or underemployed). Third, effective
decision making requires a bridging of the link between the selection
of an investment bundle and the means whereby that bundle will be
financed. This includes concern for the sources of funds to build
the projects, the optimal mix of funds from various sources, and
the optimal schedule for sequencing different phases of projects
where some discretion exists. Fourth, effective decision making
implies careful attention to the elements of plan formulation and
implementation. That is, it is not appropriate to isolate those who
conceive of projects and give them specificity from those who are
trying to incorporate them into a national plan; irrigation projects
cannot be created in the absence of concern for transportation projects, energy projects, credit projects, and other components on the
input side and on the output side from agriculture. Similarly, transportation projects cannot be conceived in isolation from agricultural

projects, and the like. This is the essence of planning, and effective
decision making in developing countries depends on this crucial in-
gredient. Finally, effective decision making depends on the availability of meaningful information. That is, we wish to draw a sharp
distinction between data as numbers and data as useful scientific
information with which to do planning for new investments and new
rules. A model for decision making must be consistent with the data
available in a country, but it can also point us in the direction of useful scientific information not now available. Put differently, there
is a short-run view of planning models and their data and a long-run
view. In the former view we must always be careful that our model
is not too far ahead of our information. On the other hand there is
a certain value in some gap as long as it leads us to acquire information of relevance which has heretofore been unavailable.

One of the first steps in improving decision making in developing
countries is to introduce explicitly the objective function of the policy
makers into our conceptual frameworks. This is not so difficult as
might seem at first blush. Countries have targets, and countries
have priorities; these represent a multidimensional objective function.
All we need to do is to incorporate these targets into our analysis
and attempt to ascertain which of several targets ranks highest. Is
job creation in one region of the country more important than foreign
exchange? If so, how far can we push this choice until the trade-offs
(in terms of foregone foreign exchange) become too dear? If it seems
difficult to obtain a clear reading of weights on alternative objectives,
it is still possible—by working interactively with the policy maker,
or by performing sensitivity analysis on our results—to present the
most likely outcomes under several assumed weights attached to the
several objectives.

Once a vector of objectives is specified, the next obvious step
is to ask what are the impacts of several means of achieving those
objectives. This information can be illustrated in several ways but
the important thing is to recognize it as an indication of the contribution of several investment alternatives to the prespecified objectives.
If a road project using one bundle of technology will create 2,000
jobs in a certain region over the next five years, then this is a different project than the same road constructed with primarily imported
tractors. The mere illustration of many of these impacts, even in
the absence of an optimizing model, can be most beneficial for the
enhancement of improved decision making.

When it comes to the economics of project financing, assuming
an ideal bundle of investments has been selected, we then must be
concerned with where the necessary capital will be obtained and how
it will be allocated to the basic components of the project(s).

A final concern arises when certain projects are included in the investment portfolio for reasons other than their inherent economic contribution. It is usually the situation that we are faced with a case in which we need to make "the best of a bad situation." Under the very real constraint on funds, the imposition of projects on purely political grounds means that otherwise good projects are unable to be undertaken. However, there are policies concerning foreign exchange rates, prices of inputs, and prices of outputs which can be altered to minimize the economic "damage" which might otherwise arise. This role of government as a rule maker to salvage otherwise "inefficient" portfolios has been rather ignored in the literature; our treatment only begins to scratch the surface.

What, then, does goal programming offer to decision makers in developing countries? As outlined in the previous chapters, GP is a systematic vector optimization approach to choice where the most common objective function is in terms of minimizing the deviations from prespecified planning targets. While it is not intended as a complete substitute for traditional benefit-cost analysis at the project level, it is the nature of a GP formulation to recognize several decision-making levels. Efficient projects at the ministerial level are assessed for their specific contribution to specific economic development targets at the macroeconomic level and are then put into an investment opportunity matrix to form a "constraint" on the optimization exercise. This hierarchical nature of the decision-making process is highlighted in the early chapters.

The presentation of the GP framework has focused on the relation of the model to the planning process and to some uses in various planning settings: selecting projects, sources of funds, and institutional alternatives to minimize the costs of politically imposed projects. We have been forced to rely on hypothetical data because our research did not permit the collection of data from an actual developing country setting. However, we view this as an advantage. Had we obtained data from an actual setting, the attention often would have been drawn to the implied relation within the economy instead of to the model as a systematic facilitator of choice. This, of course, is also a weakness in that the problem is cast in purely hypothetical terms. To us the essence of improving the planning process is the incorporation of vector optimization techniques and for this numerical examples are quite adequate for our heuristic purpose. We recognize that much work remains in developing goal programming for direct application in the developing countries. Part of this research work will necessarily involve a better integration with national-accounts models and with input-output tables constructed for nations and for regions of nations. We see goal programming as a valuable complement to these other approaches and are convinced that as the planning process moves in the direction advocated herein, the use of optimization models such as goal programming will increase.

BIBLIOGRAPHY

Adelman, I., and C. T. Morris. "An Anatomy of Income Distribution: Patterns in Developing Nations." Development Digest 9, no. 4 (October 1971): 24-37.

Anderson, H. R. "Monte Carlo Simulation." Managerial Planning, January-February 1970, pp. 26-32.

Ando, Albert, E. Cary Brown, and Ann F. Friedlaender. Studies in Economic Stabilization. Washington, D.C.: The Brookings Institution, 1968.

Arrow, Kenneth,and T. Scitovsky. Reading in Welfare Economics. Homewood, Ill.: Irwin, 1969.

Aubin, J. P. "Multi-games and Decentralization in Management." In Multiple Criteria Decision Making, ed. J. L. Cochrane and M. Zeleny. Columbia: University of South Carolina Press, 1973.

Bahroun, Sadok. "Annual Planning in Tunisia." Journal of Development Planning, no. 3 (United Nations, 1971), pp. 60-98.

Balassa, Bela et al. The Structure of Protection in Developing Countries. Baltimore: Johns Hopkins University Press, 1971.

Baldwin, Robert E. "The Case Against Infant-Industry Protection." Journal of Political Economy, May-June, 1969.

_____. Economic Development and Growth. New York: John Wiley, 1972.

Ball, R. J., et al. The International Linkage of National Economic Models. New York: North Holland-American Elsevier, 1973.

Banco Central de Chile. Estudios Monetarios II, Santiago, 1970.

Bartee, Edwin, M. "Problem Solving with Ordinal Measurement." Management Science 17, no. 10 (June 1971): 622-33.

Baryaruha, Azarias. "Factors Affecting Industrial Employment."
    Development Digest 7, no. 4 (October 1969): 17-21.

Basch, Antonin, and Milic Kybal. "Recursos Nacionales de Inversion
    en America Latina." Estudios. Mexico City: BID-CEMLA,
    1971.

Bauer, Peter T., and Basil S. Yamey. The Economics of Under-
    developed Countries. Chicago: Cambridge Economic Handbooks,
    The University of Chicago Press, 1966.

Baumol, William J. Economic Dynamics. New York: Macmillan,
    1970.

Bhagwati, Jagdish. "The Pure Theory of International Trade: A
    Survey." American Economic Association, Surveys of Economic
    Theory, Vol. 2. New York: Macmillan, 1965.

Billings, M. H., and A. Singh. "The Effect of Technology on Farm
    Employment in India." Development Digest 9, no. 1 (January
    1971): 98-107.

Blaug, Mark. "Approaches to Educational Planning." Economic
    Journal, June 1967.

Boadway, Robin. "Benefit-Cost Shadow Pricing in Open Economies:
    An Alternative Approach." Journal of Political Economy 83,
    no. 2 (1975): 419-30.

Boulding, Kenneth E. "The Economics of the Coming Spaceship
    Earth." Development Digest 9, no. 1 (January 1971): 12-15.

Bowers, David, and Robert N. Baird. Elementary Mathematical
    Macroeconomics. Englewood Cliffs, N.J.: Prentice-Hall, 1971.

Branson, William H. Macroeconomic Theory and Policy. New York:
    Harper & Row, 1972.

Bromley, Daniel W. "An Alternative to Input-Output Models: A
    Methodological Hypothesis." Land Economics 48 (May 1972):
    125-33.

____, W. B. Lord, et al. Procedures for Evaluation of Water and
    Related Land Resource Projects: An Analysis of the Water
    Resources Council's Task Force Report. Madison: Center for

Resource Policy Studies and Programs, University of Wisconsin, April 1970.

Brown, J. A. C. "A Regional Model of Agricultural Development." In The Role of Agriculture in Economic Development, ed. E. Thorbecke. New York: Columbia University Press, 1969.

Bruce, C., and J. R. Hansen. A Guide for Country Economists to the Derivation of National Parameters for Economic Project Evaluation. Washington, D.C.: The World Bank, Asia Project Department, June 25, 1973.

Bruton, Henry J. Principles of Development Economics. Englewood Cliffs, N.J.: Prentice-Hall, 1965.

Burns, T., and L. D. Mecker. "A Mathematical Model of Multi-Dimensional Evaluation, Decision-Making, and Social Interaction." In Cochrane and Zeleny.

Caves, Richard E. "Causes of Direct Investment: Foreign Firm's Shares in Canadian and United Kingdom Manufacturing Industries." Review of Economics and Statistics 56, no. 3 (August 1974): 279-93.

Chenery, H. B., and P. G. Clark. Inter-Industry Economics. New York: John Wiley, 1959.

Churman, West C. "Morality as a Value Criterion." In Cochrane and Zeleny.

Cleveland, Harlan. "The Convalescence of Foreign Aid." American Economic Review Papers and Proceedings 49, no. 2 (May 1959): 216-31.

Cline, William R. "The Potential Effect of Income Redistribution on Economic Growth in Four Latin American Countries." Development Digest 9, no. 4 (October 1971): 9-23.

Cochrane, J. L., and M. Zeleny, eds. Multiple Criteria Decision Making. Columbia: University of South Carolina Press, 1973.

Cohen, Benjamin J. Balance-of-Payments Policy. Baltimore: Penguin Books, 1970.

_____. "Foreign Exchange Constraints in Economic Development
and Efficient Aid Allocation: Comment." Economic Journal 76
(March 1966): 168–70.

Corden, M. The Theory of Protection. Oxford: Oxford University
Press, 1971.

Cukor, Gyorgy. Strategies of Industrialization in Developing Countries. New York: St. Martin's Press, 1974.

Dahlberg, Arthur O. "The Flow of National Income and Product
Diagrammed." In Selected Readings in Economics, ed. C. Lowell
Harris. Englewood Cliffs, N.J.: Prentice-Hall, 1959.

Dalkey, N., R. Lewis, and D. Snyder. Measurement and Analysis
of the Quality of Life: With Exploratory Illustrations of Applications to Career and Transportation Choices. Santa Monica,
Calif.: Rand Corporation, R-M-6228, 1970.

De Garmo, Paul E. Engineering Economy. New York: Collier-
Macmillan, 1969.

Dickert, Thomas G. "Methods for Environmental Impact Assess-
ment: A Comparison." In Environmental Impact Assessment:
Guidelines and Commentary, ed. T. G. Dickert. Berkeley:
University of California, 1974.

Dorfman, Adolfo. La Industrializacion en la America Latina y las
Politicas de Fomento. Mexico City: Fondo de Culture Economica,
1967.

Dorfman, Robert. Application of Linear Programming to the Theory
of the Firm. Berkeley: University of California Press, 1951.

_____. Measuring Benefits of Government Investments. Washington,
D.C.: Brookings Institution, 1965.

_____, P. Samuelson, and R. Solow. Linear Programming and
Economic Analysis. New York: McGraw-Hill, 1958.

Dorner, Peter. Interacciones entre los Sistemas de Tenencia de la
Tierra, la Distribucion del Ingreso y la Productividad Agricola.
Madison: University of Wisconsin, LTC Reprint No. 5-S, Land
Tenure Center, 1966.

____. "International Assistance for the Small Farmer." Challenge, May–June, 1975, pp. 62–64.

____, and J. Carlos Collarte. Land Reform in Chile: Proposal for an Institutional Innovation. Madison: University of Wisconsin, LTC Reprint No. 2, Land Tenure Center, 1965.

Dorner, P., and D. Kanel. The Economic Case for Land Reform: Employment, Income Distribution and Productivity. Madison: University of Wisconsin, LTC Reprint No. 74, Land Tenure Center, 1971.

Duesenberry, James S. "Income, Savings, and Consumption." In Selected Readings in Economics, ed. C. L. Harris. Englewood Cliffs, N.J.: Prentice-Hall, 1959.

Eckstein, Peter. Accounting Prices as a Tool of Government Planning. Cambridge, Mass.: Harvard University, Center for International Affairs, Economic Development Report No. 53, March 1967.

Economic Commission for Latin America. Economic Survey of Latin America. New York: United Nations, 1966 through 1974.

Economic Report of the President. Washington, D.C.: Government Printing Office, 1972.

Escamilla, M., G. Schramm, and F. Conzalez. "Walter as a Social Solvent? Alternative Development Strategies for Mexico's Subsistence Agricultural Sector." Congress on Water Resources, New Delhi, December 1975.

Fei, John C. H., and Gustav Ranis. "Agriculture in the Open Economy." In Thorbecke.

Feinstein, Otto,et al. "Two Worlds of Change." Reading in Economic Development. New York: Anchor Books, 1964.

Findlay, R., and S. Wellisz. Project Evaluation, Shadow Prices and Trade Policy. New York: Columbia University, Discussion Paper 74-7521, May 1975.

Forsyth, J. D., and D. J. Langhhunn. "Capital Rationing in the Face of Multiple Organizational Objectives." In Cochrane and Zeleny.

Foxley, Alejandro, and E. Garcia. "The Role of Projection in National Planning: A Methodology for Medium Term Projections and Their Application in Chile." Journal of Development Planning, no. 4 (1972), pp. 64-97.

Frank, C. R. "Public and Private Enterprise in Africa." In Government and Economic Development, ed. G. Ranis. New Haven, Conn.: Yale University Press, 1971.

Frankel, S. H. "'Psychic' and 'Accounting' Concepts of Income and Welfare." In Readings in the Concept and Measurement of Income, ed. R. H. Parker and G. C. Harcourt. Cambridge: Cambridge University Press, 1969, pp. 83-105.

Frei, Eduardo. Segundo Mensaje del Presidente de la Republica. Santiago, Chile, May 1966 and May 1977.

Freund, R. J. "The Introduction of Risk into a Programming Model." Econometrica 24 (July 1956): 253-63.

Geithman, David T. Fiscal Policy for Industrialization and Development in Latin America. Gainesville: The University Presses of Florida, 1974.

Georgescu-Roegen. "Choice, Expectations, and Measurability." Quarterly Journal of Economics 68 (1954): 503-04.

Goseco, Andres D. "Manpower Mobilization for Development." Development Digest 7, no. 4 (October 1969): 22-27.

Griffin, K., et al. Financing Development in Latin America. New York: St. Martin's Press, 1971.

Hadley, G. Linear Programming. Reading, Mass.: Addison-Wesley, 1963.

Hagen, Everett, et al. Planeacion del Desarrollo Economico. Mexico City: Fondo de Cultura Economica, 1964.

Halter, A. N., M. L. Hayenga, and T. J. Manetsch. "Simulating a Developing Agricultural Economy: Methodology and Planning Capability." American Journal of Agricultural Economics 52, no. 2 (May 1970): 272-84.

Hansen, W. Lee. "Symposium on Rates of Return to Investment in Education." Journal of Human Resources 2 (Summer 1967).

Haq, Mahbub Ul. "Annual Planning in Pakistan." Journal of Development Planning, no. 2 (1970), pp. 81-114.

_____. "Employment and Income Distribution in the 1970's: A New
Perspective." Development Digest 9, no. 4 (October 1971): 3-8.

Harberger, Arnold C. "Monopoly and Resource Allocation." American Economic Review 44, no. 2 (May 1954): 77-92.

Havens, Eugene A. Methodological Issues in the Study of Development. Madison: University of Wisconsin, LTC Reprint No. 100,
Land Tenure Center, 1972.

Hazari, B. R., and J. Krisnamurty. "Employment Implications of
India's Industrialization: Analysis in an Input-Output Framework."
Review of Economics and Statistics 52, no. 2 (May 1970): 181-86.

Heller, Robert H. International Trade Theory and Empirical
Evidence, 2d ed. Englewood Cliffs, N.J.: Prentice-Hall, 1973.

Hicks, Ursula U. Development Finance: Planning and Control.
Oxford: Oxford University Press, 1965.

Hill, Morris. "Goals-Achievement Matrix for Evaluating Alternative
Plans." Journal of the American Institute of Planners 34 (January 1964): 19-28.

Hines, G. Lawrence. Environmental Issues: Population, Pollution,
and Economics. New York: W. W. Norton, 1973.

Hirschman, Albert O. Development Projects Observed. Washington,
D.C.: Brookings Institution, 1967.

Hirshleifer, J. Investment, Interest and Capital. Englewood Cliffs,
N.J.: Prentice-Hall, 1970.

Holland, Edward P. "Discussion: Macro Simulation Models."
American Journal of Agricultural Economics 52, no. 2 (May
1970): 284-86.

Hunt, Shane. "Distribution, Growth, and Government Economic
Behavior in Peru." In Ranis.

Hurst, James W. Law and the Conditions of Freedom. Madison:
University of Wisconsin Press, 1971.

Hymer, Stephen H. "The Political Economy of the Gold Coast and Ghana." In Ranis.

International Monetary Fund. Survey of African Economies, Vols. 1 through 4. Washington, D.C., 1968.

Isard, Walter. Ecologic-Economic Analysis for Regional Development. New York: The Free Press, 1972.

Johnson, Harry. "An Economic Theory of Protection." Journal of Political Economy, June 1965.

Kaldor, Nicholas. "The Concept of Income in Economic Theory." In Readings in the Concept and Measurement of Income, ed. R. H. Parker and G. C. Harcourt. Cambridge: Cambridge University Press, 1969, pp. 161-82.

Klein, David. "The Planning Process of a Budget Agency: Form and Content." Finance and Development 8, no. 2 (June 1971): 20-25.

Kneese, A. V., R. V. Ayres, and R. C. d'Arge. Economics and the Environment: A Material Balance Approach. Baltimore: Resources for the Future, Johns Hopkins University Press, 1970.

Knetsch, J. L., R. H. Haveman, C. W. Howe, J. V. Krutilla, and M. Brewer. Federal Natural Resource Development: Basic Issues in Benefit and Cost Measurement. Washington, D.C.: Natural Resources Policy Center, The George Washington University, May 1969.

Kreinin, Mordechai E. International Economics: A Policy Approach. New York: Harcourt, Brace, Jovanovich, 1971.

Kresge, David T. "Discussion: Macro Simulation Models." American Journal of Agricultural Economics 52, no. 2 (May 1970): 288-90.

Kuznetz, S. J. "National Income as a Measure of Welfare." In Selected Reading in Economics, ed. C. L. Harris. Englewood Cliffs, N.J.: Prentice-Hall, 1959.

Land, James W. "The Role of Public Enterprise in Turkish Economic Development." In Ranis.

Laufer, Leopold. "Mutual Assistance between Developing Countries." Development Digest 6, no. 4 (October 1968): 37-43.

Leontief, W. "Environmental Repercussions and the Economic Structure: An Input-Output Approach." Review of Economics and Statistics 52, no. 3 (August 1970): 262-71.

Leopold, Luna, et al. "A Procedure for Evaluating Environmental Impact." Geological Survey, Circular 645, Washington, D.C., 1971.

Lewis, John P. "La India." In Planeacion del Desarrollo Economico, ed. E. Hagen. Mexico City, 1964.

Lewis, W. Arthur. "Employment in Nigeria." Development Digest 7, no. 4 (October 1969): 12-16.

Lipschutz, Seymour. "General Topology." Shaum's Outline Series. New York: McGraw-Hill, 1965.

Lipsey, R. "The Theory of Custom Unions: A General Survey." In Readings in International Economics, No. 16, American Economic Association.

Long, Bill L. "Identifying Environment Options in Development." Development Digest 9, no. 1 (January 1971): 34-36.

Molina, Sergio. El Proceso de Cambio en Chile. Mexico City: Siglo Veintiuno Editores, 1972.

Muraro, Gilberto. "Estimate of the Economic Damage Caused by Pollution: The Italian Experience (Comments on the ENI-ISVET Research, 1969-1970)." In Environmental Damage Costs, Organization for Economic Cooperation and Development. Paris: OECD, 1974.

Nicholls, William H. "The Transformation of Agriculture in a Presently Semi-Industrialized Country: The Case of Brazil." Thorbecke.

Nurkse, Ragner. Problems of Capital Formation in Underdeveloped Countries. New York: Oxford University Press, 1957.

Nwaneri, V. C. "Income Distribution and Project Selection." Finance and Development 10, no. 3 (September 1973): 27-29.

_____. "Income Distribution Criteria for the Analysis of Development
Projects." Finance and Development 10, no. 1 (March 1973):
17-19.

Oficina Internacional del Trabajo. Creacion de Empleo y Absorcion
de Desempleo en Chile: La Experiencia de 1971. Geneva:
International Labor Office, United Nations, 1972.

O'Hagan, J. P., and T. Lehti. "Improving the Effectiveness of
Food Aid." Development Digest 6, no. 4 (October 1968): 59-62.

Olsen, P. B., and P. N. Rasmussen. "Un Intento de Planeacion en
un Estado Tradicional: Iran." In Hagen.

Ossa, Cristian. "Annual Planning in Chile." Journal of Development
Planning, no. 6 (1974).

Ozorio, A. M. "Stockholm and the Developing Countries." Development Digest 10, no. 2 (April 1972): 18-25.

Pardee, F. S., C. T. Phillips, and K. V. Smith. Measurement and
Evaluation of Alternative Regional Transportation (Mixes).
Santa Monica, Calif.: Rand Corporation, R.M.-6324-DOT,
August 1970.

Parker, R. H., and G. C. Harcourt. Readings in the Concept and
Measurement of Income. Cambridge: Cambridge University
Press, 1969.

Pitkanen, Eero. "Goal Programming and Operational Objectives in
Public Administration." Swedish Journal of Economics 72, no. 3
(1970): 207-14.

Prebisch, Raul. "Income Distribution in Latin America: Structural
Requirements for Development." Development Digest 9, no. 4
(October 1971): 38-52.

Presidencia de la Republica. "Plan del Peru: 1971-1975." Plan
Global, Vol. 1. Lima, 1971.

_____. "Plan Nacional de Desarrollo para 1971-1975." Plan Global,
Vol. 1. Lima, 1971.

Ranis, Gustav. Government and Economic Development. New Haven,
Conn.: Yale University Press, 1971.

Reinafarje, Walter B. "Un Modelo de Simulacion para la Economia de Peru." Comercio Exterior. Mexico City: Banco Nacional de Comercio Exterior, July 1973, pp. 645-49.

Sandee, Jan. "A Programming Model for a Dual Economy." In Thorbecke.

Secretariat of the Economic Commission for Africa. "Development Planning and Economic Integration in Africa." Journal of Development Planning, no. 1 (1969), pp. 107-56.

Sfeir-Younis, Alfredo. "Multiobjective Formulation and Evaluation of Public Investments: A Model for Decision Making in Developing Countries." Ph.D. dissertation, University of Wisconsin, 1976.

Shubik, Martin. "Simulation of Industry and Firm." American Economic Review 50, no. 5 (December 1960): 908-19.

Smith, Robert D., and Paul S. Greenlaw. "Simulation of a Psychological Decision Process in Personnel Selection." Management Science 13, no. 8 (April 1967): 409-B419.

Soza, V. Hector. Planificacion del Desarrollo Industrial. Mexico City: Editorial Siglo Veintiuno, 1966.

Stewart, I. G. Economic Development and Structural Change. Edinburgh: Edinburgh University Press, 1969.

Thiesenhusen, William C. Agrarian Reform and Economic Development in Chile: Some Cases of Colonization. Madison: University of Wisconsin, LTC Reprint No. 24, Land Tenure Center, 1966.

Thorbecke, E., ed. The Role of Agriculture in Economic Development. New York: Columbia University Press, 1969.

_____, and Alfred J. Field. "Relationships between Agriculture, Nonagriculture, and Foreign Trade in the Development of Argentina and Peru." In Thorbecke.

Thornton, D. S. "Agriculture in Economic Development." Journal of Agricultural Economics 24, no. 2 (1973): 225-87.

Twiss, Robert H. "Linking the EIS to the Planning Process." In Dickert.

Tyler, William G. Income Distribution and Economic Development:
A Macro Interpretation, Paper presented to the Latin American
Studies Association Meetings, Madison, Wisc., May 3-5, 1973.

United Nations. "Conference of Human Environment." Development
Digest 10, no. 2 (April 1972): 3-4.

_____. Evaluation of Industrial Projects. Project Formulation and
Evaluation Series, Vol. 1. New York, 1968.

United Nations Economic and Social Council. "The Employment
Problem." Development Digest 7, no. 4 (October 1969): 3-11.

United Nations Panel of Experts. "Development and Environment:
The Founex Report." Development Digest 10, no. 2 (April 1972):
5-17.

Van de Wetering, Hylke. "Agricultural Planning: The Peruvian
Experience." In Thorbecke.

Ward, William A. "Employment Objectives and Agricultural Project
Appraisal: A Review of the Benefit-Cost Theory, with Research
Recommendations for Improving Application." Washington, D.C.:
International Bank for Reconstruction and Development, unpub-
lished paper, April 1974.

Williams, Fred E. "On the Evaluation of Intertemporal Outcomes."
In Cochrane and Zeleny.

Yudelman, Montague, Gurau Butler, and Ranadev Banerji. Technological Change in Agriculture and Employment in Developing
Countries. Paris: Development Centre Studies, Organization
for Economic Cooperation and Development, 1971.

acceleration principle, 5
accounts: balance-of-payments,
    11; national, 49, 77; sec-
    toral, 49
accumulation principle, 5
Adams, Richard A., 48
additive (difference) model,
    75-76
aggregation: level of, 12-14,
    80; reduced form, 17
amortization, 96

Bacha, E., 92
balance of payments, 60-61,
    103-05, 114-15; accounts,
    11; contributions to, 105;
    deficit, 143; impacts, 106;
    models, 14; pattern, 15
Balassa, Bela, 15
Baldwin, Robert H., 30
Bassoco, L. M., 159
Baumol, William J., 24, 26,
    28, 38, 40
Beattie, Bruce R., 14
benefit-cost: analysis (BCA), 2,
    12, 14-15, 17, 140, 178,
    180; ratio, 14-15, 26-27
benefit(s): present-valued, 27;
    transformation curve, 59
Bernoulli Density Function,
    151
Boehlje, Michael, 16
Bromley, Daniel W., 14
Bruno, Michael, 15, 94
budget: allocation, 10, 19-21,
    51, 61, 85; availability, 7,
    103, 129; constraint, 164;
    cycle, 123, 133; distinguish-
    able, 103; government, 19;

idle, 38; limitations, 15, 17,
    32; maximum, 17; transfers,
    39; undistinguishable, 133

Candler, Wilfred, 16
capital: absorption capacity, 116;
    average cost of, 112; budgeting,
    6, 16, 24, 30, 34, 46, 133;
    demand for, 25; domestic, 25;
    foreign, 25; opportunity cost
    of, 39, 112; optimal stock of,
    51, 115; output ratios, 4;
    productivity of, 25; rationing,
    27, 31, 33-34; stock, 103, 114,
    154; supply of, 25; wastage, 26
Carleton, Willard T., 24, 38, 40
cash flows, discounted, 25, 30,
    37
chance-constraint approach, 62,
    66
Charnes, A., 67, 70
Charnes-Stedry's Approach, 70
Chenery, Hollis G., 105
Ciriacy-Wantrup, S. V., 9
Clastorin, T. D., 140
Cohon, Jared L., 16
concessional value, 97
conjunctive: programming, 58;
    selection procedures, 58, 60-
    61
consistency principle, 5
constrained formulation, 7, 129,
    152-54
Contini, Bruno, 65
Contini's Approach, 62, 65
contract curve, 45
Cooper, W. W., 67
Courtney, J., 140
Critical Path Method (CPM), 122

currency: domestic, 102;
    foreign, 102; optimal
    mix, 6, 21, 106-19;
    transferability of, 102-19

Dean, Joel, 24-26, 30,32, 34
debt: cost of, 96; domestic, 1;
    foreign, 1, 21, 102;
    management of, 102
decision: criterion, 26; rule(s),
    26, 67, 75
degree of necessity, 25
dependency, 98
depreciation: policies, 7, 165-
    76; rate-of-accelerated,
    159-76
development: balanced, 158;
    budget, 140; contributions to,
    167; economic, 15, 80;
    goals, 13; national planning,
    17; rural, 25, 116-18, 122;
    self-sustained, 102, 117;
    targets, 19; without invest-
    ment, 5, 7
deviational variables, 49, 52-54
disbursement criteria, 123
discount rate, 35, 39, 70, 114
disjunctive: programming, 56,
    58; selection procedures,
    58, 60-61
distance function, 19, 54-56
distributionally inferior state, 2
domestic resource cost, 15, 94,
    177
dominant solutions, 61
dual evaluator, 70

ϵ-constraint, 60
effective protection, 94
efficiency: criteria, 13; economic,
    1-2, 6, 30; Pareto, 3, 4;
    production, 60
employment: generation of , 60
    127, 148-54; national, 15, 80,
    87-90; regional, 44, 61

environmental: damage, 13;
    quality, 16, 44
Evers, William H., 63, 67, 68
Evers' approach, 62, 68
exchange rate: inputs, 7, 162-76;
    outputs, 7, 162-76
executive office (EO), 10, 11
exports: foreign price of, 162-76;
    proportion of, 162-76

feasible: region, 45-46, 52-56;
    set, 59
feasibility: economic, 1, 14;
    financial, 1; fiscal, 4
finance: ministry of, 10, 11, 17;
    optimal level of, 6
financial model, 19-21
Fisher, Irving, 82-83
Fontaine, Ernesto, 95
foreign: debt, 102, 105, 115, 118;
    dependency, 105
Foreign Aid Management, 106
foreign exchange, 13, 16, 49, 80,
    90-94, 129, 143, 154; costs,
    111; earnings ratio, 15; gener-
    ation of, 94, 102-03, 127;
    markets, 102; opportunity
    cost of, 94; rate, 113, 180;
    shadow price of, 91-92;
    shortage of, 112
foreign prices: inputs, 7; outputs, 7
Frank, C. R., 96
functional space, 45-46
funds: disbursement of, 6, 21;
    domestic, 6, 17, 21;
    foreign, 6, 17, 21; sources
    of, 7, 17, 19; statistical
    attributes of, 7

goal(s): accomplishment, 7, 46-48,
    51, 61, 129-36; functions, 16-
    17; high level, 48; multiple,
    16-17, 48; overachievement of,
    48-54; programming, 6, 19,
    44-46, 61, 62, 107, 118;

underachievement of, 48, 51–54; vector, 7, 49, 62–63, 66–67, 119, 129

government: dual role of, 4, 158; as investor, 4, 158; as rule maker, 4, 158–76

grace period, 7, 95, 96, 107

grant element, 97

Gruver, G., 66, 67

Haimes, Y. Y., 60, 160

Hall, W. A., 60

Harberger, Arnold, 88, 89

Harberger-Schydlowsky-Fontaine Model, 92

Harrod-Domar Models, 116

Haveman, Robert, 86, 87

Hawkins, Clark A., 48

Heller, W. Walter, 30

Henderson, A., 33

Henderson, P. D., 26, 27, 28

Hetrick, James C., 34

Hicks, J. R., 83

hierarchical model, 158–76

Hinrichs, Harley, 2

Hirshleifer, Jack, 26

Hirshleifer Paradox, 32, 38

Ijiri, Y., 70

import: capacity, 116; marginal propensity to, 103, 105; quotas, 178; substitution, 24, 105

income: distribution of, 86–87; national, 11, 15, 16, 48, 61, 80, 82–84, 90, 103; national models, 14, 17, 77, 129; redistribution, 11, 61, 89–90, 117; regional, 15, 49, 80, 84–86, 129, 136, 143, 154; sectoral accounts, 11

input-output models, 77, 129

institutional: arrangements, 125; changes, 151, 158; level, 9; objectives, 11; principle, 5; structure, 3

Interamerican Development Bank (IDB), 61

interest rate, 7, 95, 107, 165–76

internal rate of return (IRR), 26–27, 32, 37, 111, 112–14, 140, 159

International Labor Office (ILO), 58, 61

interrelation principle, 5

investment: alternatives, 10; budget, 6; bundle, 6, 14, 31, 51, 148, 178; criteria, 15, 80, 93; financing, 17; flows, 5, 6; formulation, 76; grants, 159; optimal bundle, 6, 9, 16–19, 51, 102, 109, 129–54, 165, 179; optimal strategy, 7, 10–11, 16–19, 31, 35, 154, 158; planning process, 11; programs, 30; proposals, 10; ranking, 19, 140; selection, 16–19, 29, 44, 48; social cost of, 117; stocks, 5, 6; turnover ratio, 105

investment-opportunity matrix (IOM), 6, 17, 48, 62–63, 67, 80–94, 132, 150, 162, 167–75

iso-budget analysis, 72

iso-preference analysis, 72

Kahn, Alfred, 105

Kalter, R. J., 86

Keeney, R. L., 16, 71, 73, 75

Krueger, Anne, 15, 94

Krutilla, John V., 87

labor: shadow price of, 87, 88

lagrangian multipliers, 31, 60

land reform, 25

least-cost-criterion, 27, 28

Lee, Sang M., 47, 48, 51, 64

legislative branch, 10, 11

Levy, H., 159

lexicographic: preferences, 133; programming, 56; selection procedures, 54, 60–61, 75

Lindahl, E., 83

Little, I. M. D., 91
Lord, William B., 14
Lorie, James H., 24, 30, 32, 36, 132
Lorie-Savage Problem, 30-32

MacCrimmon, Kenneth R., 72
McGaughey, Stephen E., 15
McKean, Roland N., 14
Macko, D., 160
McLean, John G., 30
macroeconomic: accounts, 13; impacts, 6, 15, 19, 51, 143-54, 162-75; targets, 6, 13, 15, 17-21, 61, 129, 158
Madansky, A., 62, 64, 65
Major, David C., 14, 15, 59
marginal propensity of consume, 11
Marglin, Stephen, 15
marketing boards, 165
Marks, David H., 16
maturity of loans, 96, 107
Mears, Leon A., 28, 29
merit wants, 11, 54
Mikesell, Raymond, 95, 115-16, 118
Mirrlees, J. A., 91
multiobjective, 3; decision models, 6, 16, 44; evaluation, 14; linear programming, 16; utility function, 16
multiplier: effects, 143; foreign trade, 103; theory, 103

net present value (NPV), 19, 26, 37, 41, 70, 125-26, 133, 138, 143, 154, 159
Nikaido, H., 54
noninferiority, 45, 59
Norton, R. D., 159

objective(s): development, 14; economic, 11; function, 2, 19-21, 35-38, 45-48; institutional, 11; multiple, 19; national, 14; policy maker's, 15, 17-19, 44, 54; political, 11; social, 14, 17
OECD, 119
operating level, 9
optimality: Pareto, 2, 3, 45; social, 2
orthogonality, 49

Papandreou, A., 59
payoff period, 26-28
PERT, 122
plan formulation, 6
planning, Central office, 10-11, 17, 19, 49, 114, 129, 165; goals, 7; national development, 17; process, 9-10, 14
Polak, J. J., 103
policy: instruments, 165; level, 9; maker(s), 6, 11-19, 44, 48, 62, 107, 119-32, 158
preferences: direction of, 44, 51, 81; policy maker's, 119-37; transitivity of, 58; vector of, 119, 140
preferred state: potentially, 2; socially, 2, 3
price policies: foreign exchange, 162-76, 180; inputs, 180; outputs, 180; supports, 5; tariffs, 5
principal component analysis, 80, 87
programming: chance-constrained, 66; disjunctive, 56; goal, 6, 44-46, 52-56, 61-62, 118; integer nonlinear, 16; lexicographic, 58; linear, 16, 34-37, 46, 52-56, 66, 160; project-level, 17
project: attributes, 71, 72, 80; characteristics, 13; complementarity, 15, 138; components, 102, 106; cost structure, 19;

evaluators, 10-11, 17;
financing, 4, 102-27, 179;
formulation, 71, 129-57;
formulators, 10-11, 17;
implementation, 122-27;
investment structure, 107;
priorities, 6; reformulation,
159-76; selection, 51, 107,
114, 133-54; substitutes, 15,
138
projects: agricultural, 116-17,
160-76; budgeting individual,
24; contingent, 38; divisible,
36, 51, 136-38; fractional, 38;
independent, 35; indivisible,
35, 51, 140; mutually exclusive, 27-28, 37, 49, 76;
orderable, 122-27; politically
selected, 152-54; rural development, 117-18, 122; sequential, 50, 62; "shelf of," 125,
178; subordinate, 50
projections: national accounts, 17;
regional accounts, 17; sectoral accounts, 17

Quandt, Richard E., 24, 38, 40

ratio: benefit-cost, 14-15, 26,
28; foreign-exchange earnings, 15; labor-investment,
15; output-investment, 15
reduced cost method, 143
Reina, R., 116
repayment capacity, 1, 103,
109, 113
rights, 3, 5; neutral, 4; perverse, 4

Sachs, Ignacy, 13
sacrifice principle, 5
Samuelson, Paul A., 3
Sarnat, M., 159
satisficing solution, 46, 51, 52
Savage, Leonard J., 24, 30, 32,
36

scalarization, 19, 45
Schlaifer, Robert, 33, 75
Schmid, A. Allan, 14, 86
Selowsky, Marcelo, 95
Sengupta, J. K., 66, 67
sensitivity analysis, 19, 134,
148-50
shadow: price, 36-37, 88; profits,
161-75; value, 32
Silos, J. S., 159
Simons, H. C., 84
simplex method, 56
Siwijatmo, J. B. D., 28, 29
Social: benefits from financing,
125; cost of financing, 111-12;
goals, 6; objectives, 19, 60-
61; productivity, 15; time preference, 40; welfare, 83; welfare
function, 2, 16, 76
source-of-funds matrix, 7, 62,
63, 81, 94-97, 107, 119, 133
Stedry, A., 70
Steiss, A. W., 9
Stevens, Thomas, 86
stochastic, 63
surrogate worth trade off, 60

target groups, 3
Taylor, L., 92
Thorbecke, Erick, 15
Tversky, A., 75, 76

uncertainty solutions, 44, 62-70,
150; chance-constraint, 62,
66-69; Charnes-Stedry, 62,
69-70; Contini, 62, 65-66;
Evers, 62, 67-69; expected-
value, 62-63; "fat," 62, 64, 67;
"slack," 62, 64-65
unconstrained formulation, 154
United Nations, 132
United Nations Development Pro-
gramme (UNDP), 61
United Nations Industrial Development Organization (UNIDO), 87,
89, 90, 92, 93

utility: approach, 71; function, 75, 77

vector: goal, 49, 67, 179; optimization, 44ff; of weights, 62-63

Warren, Robert A., 30
Waterston, Albert, 84
weights, 15, 19, 21; vector of, 19, 50

Weingartner, H. M., 24, 32, 33, 34, 37, 38, 132
welfare criterion: Kaldor-Hicks, 2; potential compensation, 2; Scitovsky, 2, 3
welfare function, 71, 73, 107
working rules, 5

Zohar, U., 59

ABOUT THE AUTHORS

ALFREDO SFEIR-YOUNIS is currently an economist at the World Bank. He entered the Bank's Young Professionals Program after receiving his doctorate at the University of Wisconsin in 1976. Dr. Sfeir-Younis is a native of Chile, where he received a B.A. in economics and a Commercial Engineer's degree from the University of Chile before coming to the United States. He has taught mathematical statistics at the University of Chile and economics at both the Catholic University of Chile in Santiago and the Catholic University in Valparaiso. His research interests focus on public decision making and natural resource economics related to economic development in the developing countries.

DANIEL W. BROMLEY is Professor in the Department of Agricultural Economics and Director of the Center for Resource Policy Studies and Programs, University of Wisconsin, Madison. He has been on the Wisconsin faculty since 1969, when he received his Ph.D. in natural resource economics from Oregon State University. Professor Bromley is the coauthor of two books and has published numerous articles on public decision making in the natural resource field. He is also editor of the journal Land Economics. He has been a consultant to the U.S. Water Resources Council, the National Commission on Water Quality, the U.S. Army Corps of Engineers, the Natural Resource Economics Division of the U.S. Department of Agriculture, the Texas Water Development Board, and the Institute of Urban and Regional Research at the University of Iowa. During the 1973-74 academic year he spent six months with the office of the secretary, U.S. Department of the Interior, and six months with the Division of Economics and Sector Planning in the Agency for International Development. In the latter position he was a consultant to AID regarding natural resources in general, and AID-funded fishery programs in Brazil, Panama, El Salvador, and Guatemala. He also has been working with AID and the government of the Dominican Republic on water management problems in that country.

*DEVELOPMENT WITHOUT DEPENDENCE
Pierre Uri

*PATTERNS OF POVERTY IN THE THIRD WORLD:
A Study of Social and Economic Stratification
Charles Elliott, assisted by
Francoise de Morsier

PLANNING FOR ECONOMIC DEVELOPMENT: The
Construction and Use of a Multi-Sectoral Model for
Tunisia
Oli Hawrylyshyn

TAXATION AND DEVELOPMENT
edited by N. T. Wang

THE USE OF INDEXATION IN DEVELOPING
COUNTRIES
G. Donald Jud

*Also available in paperback as a PSS student edition.